GLOW ANYWAY

The Inside-Out Path to Taking Your Power Back After Hitting Rock Bottom

Nikki Kraus

Glow Anyway: The Inside-Out Path to Taking Your Power Back After Hitting Rock Bottom

For permission requests, contact:
Support@glowwithnikki.com

First Edition

Printed in the United States of America

Dedication

To Leilani and Lillian—my living poems,
the art that saved me

To Ma—your strength built me

To Daddy—I carry your heart

To Krys—you've been right all along

Foreword

This isn't just a book, it contains the essence of a juggernaut. Within it rests a timeless, repeatable, scalable template that has the power to recalibrate one's trajectory and gift them the ability to manifest the life of their dreams. Much of the blood, sweat, and tears that could have otherwise been part of someone's story can be bypassed.

The word emotion means energy in motion. Truth has a resonance and authenticity is the highest of human emotional frequencies. Energy is transferred whether spiritually, mentally, emotionally, or physically, and all bodies are connected. The reader will feel the raw potency of every word in its depth and sincerity and be touched, changed for the better because of it. They will see glimpses of themselves and what is possible if they follow through with insight and clarity. An honest, heart-on-sleeve approach is grounds for true transformation to develop.

It is necessary to start an intentional journey with the raw materials—not what we wish something was or pretend it to be because then we are living a life of dis-ILL-usion. We cannot build brick-and-mortar castles that stand the test of time with flimsy, synthetic components. Similarly, in life, we must look at things for what they truly are to know what we are actually working with to be able to create the most solid outcomes.

In true Nikki fashion, she jumps straight to the heart of matters with the skill and precision of an experienced samurai warrior. We watch as she alchemizes her pain into purpose from a young age into adulthood, in turn sharing her knowledge with the world. Embracing life's extreme difficulties head-on and clearing paths of inner-me's—triggers and self-opposition—she equips herself with the ability and tools to move forward with grace. Our everyday woman self-made into magnificent wholeness, she epitomizes what it means to catapult oneself into their royal birthright, turning lead into gold.

Born in the South Side of Milwaukee, Wisconsin, Nikki was raised there surrounded by a large extended family of Red Lake Band of Chippewa Natives, herself being a tribal member. With some of her European bloodline scattered throughout, her existence conjoined two completely different worlds and became the foundation on how Nikki became a bridge to both.

Rampant alcoholism running on both sides of her family, the odds were stacked against her that she may one day end up on the same path. After taking her first drink as a teenager this began a toxic habit, one which she would only lay to rest thanks to the blissing of parenthood. Around the age of fourteen she moved to a small, rural town named Waynesboro, Virginia. There she sustained cultural shock and remained for three years until moving just outside of Phoenix, Arizona to a city named Anthem.

It was around this time that she became closely associated with military life, eventually becoming an Airman of The United States Air Force herself. She was married to her husband, also a fellow Airman, for a total of fifteen years. Together, they traveled the world and conceived two beautiful daughters together. After a long time of trying to work things out between them, she made the heart-wrenching decision to leave. While swimming through the torrential waters of divorce, she successfully navigated and built a new life from the bottom up. Incorporating a newfound focus on spiritual growth and personal development she quickly evolved by leaps and bounds, establishing a drastically new self, identity, and vision in less than two years.

She became a certified life-coach, creating her signature GLOW framework, and entered into the realm of entrepreneurship. Her mission is centered around The Most High, faith, and radical responsibility. Currently located in Las Vegas, Nevada, her priorities are lovingly and consciously parenting her two young daughters while leaving them a legacy, coaching, and wealth building for the Kingdom.

My name is Krystal Kraus. I am Nikki's only sibling and older sister. We are close in age and because of it shared many experiences together. Her upbringing was my upbringing but who I am and my credentials are irrelevant. What is important is the fact that this book was created to be a voice for those who never got the chance to be heard as well as service to humanity because we have come to the time for us to rise collectively as a species.

Nikki and I's life has always been extraordinary in some way, shape, or form, and from a young age there was almost always something of sheer importance or seriousness. Now we know that we were being put through the 'Bootcamp of Life'. In hindsight, we didn't realize the extent of just how consequential everything was. It was so much bigger than all of us and for a purpose far greater than most have still yet to realize.

As I grew older, I noticed a pattern—many people who reach their full potential and splendor come from challenging or even troubled backgrounds. I innerstand now that some of life's most precious gems and pearls of wisdom are unveiled and obtained in the darkness. Creation's most sacred treasures are buried in the most unexpected places—priceless gifts that touch our hearts and souls in ways that not only bestow us with the strength to continue moving forward—but ignite a fire deep within that has the potential to spread as far as people are willing to pass the torch.

I implore you, the reader, to take calculated risks on yourself starting now. There is no time but the present. Where there is a will there is always a way and with repetitive, meticulously applied action, anything is possible when we put our minds to it.

Table of Contents

Introduction:
I've Been Where You Are

Let me tell you about the night I held death in my hands.

I woke up on my kitchen floor to the stench of rotting takeout and shame. The empty Jack Daniel's bottle was still warm in my hand, my ex's gun sitting on the counter.

I almost became a statistic.

I was a military-trained weather forecaster prepared to predict incoming storms, but I missed the Category 5 hurricane wrecking my own life.

My apartment looked like depression had moved in and redecorated. Days of sauce-stained takeout containers stacked like corpses; empty bottles stood guard, keeping my trauma company while I spiraled into places I swore I'd never go.

Maybe I'm better off gone. No real friends. No joy. A neglectful husband who treated my heart like a dumping ground.

The night before, I'd been swigging ZzzQuil. Almost half the bottle was already in me. I knew better than to mix alcohol and sleep aids, but something in me had said screw it hours ago. My ex was gone on a work trip, and I was drowning in my own head, alone in that little ~~prison~~ apartment.

I was loaded, the gun was loaded, and I was tossing it around like it was a toy. In my pharmaceutical fog, I accidentally racked a round into the chamber and couldn't figure out how to clear it. If I'd been sober, no problem. But I wasn't sober. I was spinning, heavy, fading off into sleep with a weapon in my hands.

That was my last memory before I blacked out. I don't remember putting it down. It felt like it weighed a thousand pounds. And I didn't care.

I'd been living by someone else's design for so long, convinced I couldn't change. But the second I started breaking away, I realized something that would save my life: I'd had the power all along.

Why This Book Exists

I'm not here to sell you another morning routine or teach you how to manifest your dream life with vision boards and positive affirmations.

I'm not going to remind you that everything happens for a reason (even though it does) or that you just need to think differently about your problems (even though you do).

This book exists because I needed it that night, and it didn't exist.

I needed someone to grab me by the shoulders and say, *"Listen, you're not a lost cause. You're just running the wrong program."*

I needed someone to tell me that I wasn't destined for failure. I needed a voice that said it's okay to grieve. It's okay to mourn. Hold a funeral for the past if you need to.

But when the tears have drained you, when the weight feels too heavy to carry any longer, that's your cue.

Let it go. Stand up. Shake yourself off. Glow anyway.

Remember when you were a kid and you needed your parents to sign a permission slip before you could go on that field trip? Without their signature, you had to stay behind while everyone else got on the bus.

Well, I'm not your parent, but I'm about to hand you something even more powerful: Permission to live your own dream life.

Right now, I'm signing off on things no one else has been brave enough to authorize:

Permission to not have it all together. To drop the performance and stop pretending "fine" is enough.

Permission to choose yourself without explaining your choices to anyone. No defense required.

Permission to drop the hand-me-down identities written by family cycles, society, religion, and systems that never had your best interests at heart.

Permission to feel the anger, the grief, the chaos, and not rush past it, but rather use it as fuel for the fire that's going to burn down everything fake in your life.

Permission to believe that the mess you've been carrying isn't weakness. It's evidence that you're still here, still standing, still fighting.

Nobody told me I could just stop.

Stop pretending "fine" was enough. Stop wearing exhaustion like a badge of honor. Stop drinking poison to feel likable. Stop shrinking so people would stay comfortable around me.

Nobody said, "Hey, you can quit that game anytime you want."

So I kept playing by the rules that were killing me, thinking I had no choice.

I wish someone had shoved this truth in my face years earlier: You don't need to earn rest. You don't need to earn joy. You don't need to earn belonging.

You're enough, exactly as you are, right now. Take you as is or leave you alone.

If you're reading this book, your permission slip is signed.

Your Glow-Up Awaits

Life won't stop throwing punches, but you don't have to take them lying down.

The real work begins when you're standing right in the middle of the wreckage of your old life.

When your family calls you selfish for choosing yourself. When your friends get uncomfortable because you're no longer the one who fixes everyone else's problems.

Most people fold here. They decide that familiar misery beats new opportunity and crawl back into the cage they came out of.

But you didn't pick up this book because you wanted it easy. You picked it up because something inside you is screaming that there has to be more.

Well, there is.

Most people think of a "glow-up" as an Instagram-scroll-stopping flurry of photos that make your high school crushes drool. But the truth is, real glow-ups happen in places nobody posts about.

On shower floors at 9 a.m., when you realize you can't keep living like this. When you decide to stop numbing yourself into oblivion. Standing in front of a mirror, choosing to be hated for who you are rather than loved for who you're pretending to be.

Let's get one thing straight: Glowing anyway is *not* some feel-good quote slapped on a coffee.

This is brutal work. Shoulders back, chest out, chin up—you own the collapse, the chaos, the absolute disorder of your life, and you stand tall anyway.

Your glow has nothing to do with having it all together and everything to do with refusing to let rock bottom have the last word over your life.

I know what this feels like because I've lived it. Holding the weight of heartbreak, fear, exhaustion, and doubt, but letting the deeper me shine through anyway.

Something they couldn't kill, no matter how hard they tried. It's quiet, not flashy. A calm whisper that says, "Yes, I fell. But I got back up, and this time I chose me."

When the Method Found Me (Through Green Juice and Pure Stubbornness)

Lightning-bolt moments make for great movies, but most of life doesn’t work that way. Mine crept in through the most ordinary thing—making green juice while the rest of my life felt upside down.

After I left the family house when I separated from my ex, I took a job as a gas station manager to get back on my feet after years as a stay-at-home mom. I was working long hours, grabbing convenience food because it was easy, surviving on caffeine, and dragging the constant stress of a messy divorce behind me. Whatever free time I had was consumed by problems I didn’t know how to solve. Then my skin started breaking out badly, and I knew it wasn’t random—it was my body sounding the alarm.

At first, I tried creams and products, hoping to treat it from the outside in. But deep down, I knew better. My body was begging for real nourishment, not another band-aid fix. I wasn't fueling or hydrating myself properly, and intuitively I knew I needed to reset from the inside out.

So, I bought a juicer. Not because it was trendy, but because I was ready to make a conscious shift. Juicing isn't convenient—seven pieces to clean, pulp all over the counter—but I treated it as a non-negotiable. Apple. Cucumber. Celery. Whenever I found a pocket of time, I made the juice. Before long, it became more than a habit. It became a daily ritual—a small act of discipline that reminded me I had control over at least one piece of my life.

By week six, I started seeing visible results. My skin cleared. My natural energy returned as I cleaned up my diet, drastically scaled back caffeine, and finally gave my body the hydration it had been begging for.

It wasn't about chasing some miracle. It was about consistency—showing up for myself again and again, even when it was inconvenient. Each glass was a reminder that I was rebuilding from the inside out, giving my body what it truly needed instead of running on fumes.

And the shift reached deeper than just clearer skin or renewed energy. For the first time in years, I felt what it was like to fuel myself with intention, to nurture instead of neglect. A quiet glow began to rise from within—not just in my reflection, but in how I carried myself, how I moved through the day, how I chose what mattered.

That's when it clicked. This was bigger than green juice. I was clearing out what was weighing me down, creating steadiness where there had been chaos, and giving myself the foundation to thrive. And I realized I had done this before, many times—by rebuilding myself at the root. I just hadn't recognized the pattern until then.

Your Roadmap Through the Fire

This book is divided into three parts, and each one is going to take you somewhere different. Somewhere necessary.

Part One is called "Before the Glow" because we're going straight into the dark night of your soul. We're talking about the familiar patterns that are literally killing you slowly, why you cling to them anyway, and what it really looks like when your life is in slow collapse while you're still pretending everything is fine.

I'm going to show you why hitting rock bottom might actually be the best thing that ever happened to you. Fair warning: This part gets real.

Part Two hands you the GLOW Method in full detail, but here's what I'm not going to do. I'm not going to give you some surface-level explanation and send you on your way. We're going deep.

- **G**rowth means facing the brutal, unfiltered truth about where you are and who you're becoming. Not who everyone else thinks you should be.

- **L**ove means treating yourself like someone you actually love. Instead of someone you're constantly trying to fix, improve, or apologize for.
- **O**vercome means breaking those old patterns and healing what's been stored in your body for years. Even when it gets messy and uncomfortable and makes people squirm.
- **W**isdom means turning your pain into purpose and designing a life you don't want to escape from. Not just one that looks good on social media.

Part Three is where we build a life you don't want to escape from. We're talking about what happens when you start living out loud, when people don't recognize you anymore, when you have to deal with the inevitable backslides and resistance.

The work doesn't end when you start glowing. It evolves. And we're going to talk about what that really looks like when the Instagram filters come off.

Throughout all three parts, you're going to discover things about yourself that might surprise you. Why you've been choosing the same pain over and over. How your childhood wired you for patterns that no longer serve you. How to redesign those patterns instead of just trying to think your way out of them. And what it actually means to glow anyway when your life is still messy and imperfect.

The Promise and the Lifeline

Here's my promise to you. This book will be the lifeline I wish I'd had when I was drowning in my own patterns. Not another manual telling you to think positively or manifest your way out of trauma. Not another guru promising you can heal everything with good vibes and essential oils.

This is the voice that says it's okay to fall apart completely before you come back together. The voice that tells you your mess is not your fault, but your healing is your responsibility. The voice that reminds you that you've survived 100% of your worst days so far, and that's not an accident.

I promise you'll understand why you keep choosing the same pain and how to finally set yourself free. Why your rock bottom moments weren't signs of your weakness but evidence of your strength. How to stop living the same year on repeat and start designing a life that fits who you're actually becoming.

Most importantly, I promise you'll know you're not alone in this. Every story I share, every truth bomb I drop, every moment of brutal honesty in these pages is me saying: I've been where you are, and there's a way through.

This book exists because you exist. Because your story matters. Because your healing matters. Because the world needs the version of you that emerges when you finally stop playing small.

PART ONE:
BEFORE THE GLOW — THE DARK NIGHT

Chapter 1:
The Familiar Is Killing You

Third trimester, 295 pounds, standing in my bathroom, taking selfies I never wanted anyone to see.

My ex-husband was somewhere in Kuwait on deployment. He wouldn't meet our daughter until she was three months old. I was 35 and a half weeks pregnant, alone, documenting a moment that should have been pure joy but felt like pure punishment.

I couldn't bring myself to hire a photographer because I was so disgusted with what I'd become.

But let me back up. This isn't really a weight story.

This is about the day I came face-to-face with a woman I didn't recognize. A woman who had my name, my memories, my stretch marks, but none of my soul.

I'd always been 165 pounds. Steady, predictable, comfortable in my own skin. Now I was staring at someone who had gained 130 pounds of everything I'd been too afraid to say out loud.

The camera on my phone felt heavy in my hands. Each photo felt like evidence in a trial where I was both the defendant and the judge.

Where had I gone? When had I decided that making everyone else comfortable was worth making myself invisible?

My daughter was going to be born any day. And I realized with a clarity that cut through all my excuses that if I didn't change, this is what she'd learn about being human. That we shrink ourselves. That we apologize for taking up space. That we smile while we suffocate.

The woman in those photos—she smiled for the camera, she carried my child, she lived in my house. But she had forgotten something crucial: how to choose herself.

I took thirty-seven photos that day. Deleted thirty-six of them. Kept one as evidence of the woman who refused to stay.

That bathroom mirror became my line in the sand. Not because of the number on the scale, but because of the emptiness behind my eyes. I'd spent so many years bending myself into shapes that fit everyone else's comfort zones that I'd forgotten I had a shape of my own.

Three days later, I had my daughter in an emergency C-section. The first time I held her, I made a promise that took me two more years to keep: she would never see her mother disappear the way I had.

This is where my story really begins. Not with the weight gain, but with the weight of finally seeing who I'd become when I stopped being myself.

The Script I Knew by Heart

The pattern that nearly killed me started with a simple rule: Keep everyone happy.

Don't rock the boat. Don't upset anyone. Don't make things harder than they already are. I knew this script by heart because I'd been rehearsing it since childhood.

It looked like control at first. Like I was managing everything, holding it all together. Really, it was draining the life out of me one "yes" at a time. I woke up every day carrying everyone else's needs while mine got smaller and smaller. I said "yes" when I wanted to scream "no." I smiled when I wanted to cry. I made myself small so no one else had to feel uncomfortable.

I've always been "too much." Too loud, too intense, too honest, too emotional. So I learned to dim that light for everyone else's comfort. The dimmer I got, the more people seemed to like me. The more they liked me, the more I thought I was doing something right.

That's the deception patterns play on you. They make you think they're protecting you when all they're really doing is shrinking you. Familiarity whispers that survival is enough, but it's not. I wasn't safe. I was trapped in a life that didn't even feel like mine. Suffocating under the weight of what I thought I "had" to do to be loved.

What's Your Script?

Take a moment here. What's the script you know by heart? What are the unspoken rules you follow without question? The ones that feel so automatic you don't even notice them anymore?

Maybe yours sounds like:

- "Don't be too much."
- "Don't ask for too much."
- "Don't expect too much."
- "Work harder than everyone else to prove you belong."
- "Fix everyone's problems so they'll need you."
- "Stay quiet to keep the peace."

These scripts feel like truth because we've been living them so long. But they're just programs someone else wrote for us. And programs can be rewritten.

A Forty-Ounce Childhood

Between the ages of nine and thirteen—the years when childhood innocence begins to give way to awareness—I was already learning lessons that would shape me for a lifetime. Those were the years that honed my matriarchal and nurturing disposition, the traits I continue to carry through everything I do. And it wasn't by accident. It was because of my parents—two very different people who, in their own ways, taught me how to love, how to give, how to survive.

I come from a family of love, empathy, and an alcoholic father. My dad, for all his struggles, was a spiritual billionaire. He was the humblest man you could ever meet—rich in compassion even when he was broke. He carried the happiness and pure spirit of a child, a lightness that couldn't be dimmed by circumstance. He had character and generosity that could never be measured in money.

If he had only a few coins in his pocket—the ones he'd been saving for his 40oz of cheap malt liquor—he'd still hand them to the stranger sitting outside a store asking for change, certain they needed it more than he did. Then he'd sit right beside them, swapping stories like they'd been old buddies. We'd tug on his arm, whispering, "Dad, we have to go now," and he'd hug them before parting ways. That was my dad—warm, magnanimous, magnetic. But he was also tethered to a bottle he could never let go of.

In the end, he couldn't survive without it. If he stopped drinking, his body would betray him. And so the bottle never left his side. If you saw my dad, you probably saw a King Cobra tucked close by—hidden in closets, under sinks, even behind headstones at the cemetery where he worked. He called my mom, my sister, and me his "three coo coo kitties." We were his girls. But when my mom finally left, his spirit broke, and that was the beginning of the end for him.

My mom, though, was and still is the rock of our family. She taught me what it means to love fiercely, to keep giving even when you think you've reached the end of yourself. Inventive, grounded, savage—she could fix anything, solve any problem, hold everything together with grit and empathy. The one you wanted on your team. Many days she worked double shifts as a program coordinator at a group home for people with physical and mental disabilities, carrying the weight my dad dropped.

I remember my sister and I always walking four blocks to the bus stop after school, taking it 58 streets up to visit her at work. To us, it was like stepping into another world. We watched her move through that place with ease, calling people by name, making them laugh, calming their fears. Where others might have seen limitations, she saw possibilities. Where others might have turned away, she leaned in closer.

She carried herself with strong morals and unwavering ethics, always holding firm to what was right, even when it wasn't easy. She was a protector by nature—shielding not only us, her daughters, but also the people entrusted to her care. If someone needed a voice, she spoke. If someone needed an advocate, she showed up. She showed us how to kneel to meet someone's eyes, how to listen with patience when words came slowly, how to see the person first and not the diagnosis.

There was no judgment in her presence, only steadiness, kindness, and respect. For us as kids, those afternoons were lessons you couldn't learn in school. We learned that every human being deserves dignity. That love isn't selective. That strength isn't just about how much you can carry, but how gently you can carry someone else.

Those visits shaped me more than I realized at the time. Watching her navigate a world so many overlook taught me that leadership can look like service, that true power is protective, principled, and deeply human. She didn't just raise us at home—she raised us there too, showing us what it means to be unwavering and soft, ethical and brave, a mother and a shield all at once. Watching her hold the world together with determination shaped how I saw strength.

That was the backdrop of my childhood—chaos hiding in plain sight, dressed up to look like "normal." At home, I was safe, though my mom's voice often rose as she pleaded with my dad to stop drinking or when she was reprimanding my sister and me for staying out past our curfew. The real turbulence came from my wider family—the ones who stirred trouble when alcohol got the best of them. Sometimes it was in groups, sometimes it was just one person spiraling on their own, but either way, I felt the weight of responsibility.

I learned early that if I could keep people calm, maybe things wouldn't escalate. My nervous system became a radar, tuned in to the smallest shifts in tone or body language. I molded myself into whatever version of me might keep the peace in that moment. That survival wiring stuck—it became both my armor and my prison.

And outside our four walls, the south side of Milwaukee, Wisconsin, carried its own weight. The air was thick with gangs, assumptions, and violence. It didn't matter who we really were—people decided for us based on where we lived, who we hung around, or what side of the street we walked on. Guns tucked into waistbands like accessories, drugs exchanged in plain sight, fights breaking out without warning. The parties that seemed glamorous were just another stage for destruction. Skipping school felt routine—not because we didn't care about our future, but because the pull of the streets was louder than the voice telling us to sit in a classroom. It was chaos we never asked for, cycles of poverty, addiction, and survival that started long before us.

At fourteen, everything shifted. My mom made the choice to leave, and though I know now she was doing the best she could with what she had, the fallout hit me hard. By then, school in Milwaukee had already slipped through my fingers. I failed my first year of 9th grade—not because I couldn't do the work, but because I wasn't showing up. I was chasing parties, numbing myself in any way I could. At that age, I thought I was living. In truth, I was already running.

The move to Waynesboro, Virginia, didn't bring relief—it only layered new trauma on top of old wounds. Overnight, everything familiar was gone. The safety net I didn't even realize I had was ripped away, and in its place came more instability, more weight on shoulders already too young to carry it. Virginia forced me to face the reality that "normal" could unravel in an instant and that survival would demand even more of me than before.

And yet, buried inside the pain, Virginia gave me something unexpected: a fresh academic leaf. For the first time in years, I stopped skipping class. I showed up. I studied. I proved to myself I could succeed. That momentum carried me forward when I eventually moved to Phoenix with my auntie and uncle—my mother's sister and her husband—to finish my last year of high school. There, I kept pushing, graduated strong, and walked away with a 3.9 GPA. Being pulled out of Milwaukee—the noise, the gangs, the endless distractions—gave me the chance to write a different ending to my high school story, one I'll be forever grateful for.

But even as I succeeded in the classroom, survival was still about more than grades. It meant reading the room before I stepped into it, studying body language like flashcards, anticipating needs before they were ever spoken. I became adaptable, intuitive—the kind of person who could walk into any space and instantly know who needed what. But the cost was silence inside myself. I was so busy listening to everyone else's signals that I forgot how to hear my own voice.

That's what those years gave me—resilience wrapped in hyper-awareness, strength bound with softness, a heart trained to love and to protect. Milwaukee scarred me. Virginia scarred me again. But both carved me into someone who could stand, who could carry, who could keep moving—even when the ground kept shifting.

DNA Deep Trauma

As I zoom out, I can see this wiring didn't begin with me. It didn't even begin with my parents. My ancestry is the meeting of two very different bloodlines, each carrying its own history, its own weight.

On my father's side—mostly German with threads of other European roots—the shadows ran deep. He was the son of alcoholics, and that inheritance gripped him early. By the time he had a family of his own, the bottle had him completely. I wasn't close to that side, yet their choices still touched me, like echoes passing through glass walls. I hold respect for where he came from, for the strength and lineage that still flows in me. But it was my mother's side—the Native side—that shaped me most. Or maybe, more honestly, it was the trauma of my mother's side that left the deepest mark.

My maternal family is Native American; my great-grandparents were Chippewa from the Red Lake Indian Reservation in Northern Minnesota. That land is both beautiful and heavy, carrying pride and pain in equal measure. It is where my bloodline begins, where culture and survival sit side by side, where the scars of genocide still live in the quiet corners of memory.

We are a people who endured the stripping of language, the severing of tradition, the weight of poverty, and the grip of alcoholism—wounds not born from weakness, but from centuries of policies designed to erase us. My family is proof of both the suffering and the survival. To come from Red Lake is to inherit not only a name, but a history—one forged in resilience, oppression, and the unyielding truth that we are still here.

My great-grandmother was born in 1922. As a child, she was taken from her home and forced into an Indian boarding school. They cut her hair, stripped her language, and punished her for her traditions. They tried to sever her from her people, her culture, her very identity. That kind of violence doesn't stop with one person—it leaves wounds so deep they carry forward into the generations that follow. We'll never know what happened to her parents, or their parents before them. Their stories were never written down, yet they still live in the marrow of our bones.

My great-grandfather was born in 1921. He was drafted into World War II and sent to Europe as an Army medic. On the front lines, he saved the lives of his brothers-in-arms, patched wounds under fire, and carried soldiers back from the brink of death. His language was used for war, his body for service. And in 1945, he returned home on the Queen Elizabeth, but not all of him made it back. He never spoke of the things he saw, but silence can be as heavy as words. Part of him remained on those battlefields, and that unspoken weight trickled down, shaping the way love and fear were carried in our family.

They were the ones who stood at the head of our family–the ones who raised my mother, who is 100% Native, half

Chippewa, and half Assiniboine Sioux. My sister and I are proud to be enrolled members of the Red Lake Band of Chippewa Indians, carrying that lineage forward as a quarter Native. Our tribe is more than bloodlines; it is survival embodied, culture preserved despite everything designed to erase it. This book, in part, is my way of putting Red Lake on the map–of speaking our story into the light, of naming what so many Native families have carried quietly in their DNA.

Because genocide doesn't only happen in massacres and wars—it happens in classrooms where Native children were beaten for speaking their language, in homes fractured by forced assimilation, in generations bound by poverty, addiction, and the aftershocks of stolen identity. It happens quietly, in the patterns we inherit, in the pain that arrives long before we even know who we are.

By the time it reached my mom, she tried her best to dam the river, to keep the pain from flooding into me and my sister. But the current was strong. There was too much alcohol woven through our family lines, too many unhealed wounds, too many unspoken stories passed down like invisible heirlooms. She guarded us the best she could, but trauma always finds the cracks.

This is the inheritance of my bloodline—strength and suffering, resilience and devastation. A family tree rooted in Red Lake, watered by sacrifice, bent under the weight of war and addiction. It runs through my veins. It explains so much of who I became, and why healing—real, generational healing—has become not just my path, but my responsibility.

Research shows that trauma literally changes our DNA. Studies have found that children and grandchildren of trauma survivors carry altered stress responses—traces of fear, grief, and survival coded into their cells before they ever take their first breath. Scientists call it epigenetic inheritance—the truth that our ancestors' experiences don't just live in stories, they live in us.

So when I say I was wired for alcoholism, I mean it literally. It was in my blood, in my environment, in the history I inherited. By the time I was grown, it didn't feel like a coping skill anymore. It felt like my identity.

That's how deep patterns run. They thread themselves through the body, move quietly beneath the skin, and drift like currents into the next generation. They don't start with us, and they don't end with us—unless someone decides to break them.

The Uniform That Couldn't Hide the Truth

The second most notable pattern I broke after alcoholism was my marriage to an Air Force senior NCO (non-commissioned officer). I convinced myself the stability was worth the misery. He was on active duty, which meant steady pay, benefits, housing. On paper, it looked like security. In reality, it was another cage with better decorations.

Speaking truth invited judgment. Sharing my feelings meant being told I was too emotional, too sensitive, too much. So I learned to swallow my truth and perform the role of the perfect military wife. Keep the home running smoothly. Don't complain about the deployments. Don't rock the boat when he comes home and expect everything to revolve around his schedule. From the outside, we looked perfect—a power couple in uniform, a well-oiled machine. I was the ace up his sleeve, the one who made sure the picture stayed spotless while he wore the shine. But the uniform couldn't hide the truth: behind closed doors, there was no intimacy, no tenderness, no love that reached me where I needed it most.

I cried myself to sleep in a loveless marriage. Night after night, I lay beside a man who treated me like an obligation, not a choice. He dimmed my light for years, convincing me I was always too loud, too alive. So I sat down. I went quiet. I learned to make myself small because that's what his stoicism demanded. Affection was rationed. Kisses rare. Nights ended with nothing more than a handhold. That was supposed to be enough.

I told myself I'd made my bed, so I had to lie in it. That this was the path I had chosen, so I didn't get to complain when it hurt. I thought I was stuck with it. I truly believed I was broken, unworthy, not good enough for anything better. But at the same time, I knew there was more in me. I knew I had value, talent, and real-life experience. I just didn't know how to believe it enough to actually do something with it.

The crazy part is that the suffering almost felt safe. I knew what to do with pain. I knew how to get through it. But joy? Peace? Feeling whole? That was terrifying, because I didn't trust it to last. There was nobody truly solid I could confide in. Not even my husband, because being honest only brought more criticism.

Years of living like that takes a toll. They stain your soul, whispering that maybe this is all you'll ever have, that stability matters more than joy, that safety is worth the silence. You can survive in the dark, but living requires light. No camouflage could cover the emptiness of a home where love had long gone missing.

The Lies That Whisper At Night

If my patterns had voices back then, they would have whispered the most sinister lies:

- "Don't move. Don't risk it. You'll end up alone."
- "Better to settle than to lose everything."
- "This is as good as it gets."
- "No one else will want you."
- "You'll wish you stayed."
- "At least here you have something."

For too long, I believed the voices. I had fire in me, but no faith. I didn't even know what faith was at the time. It took me years to see the lie.

Your patterns have voices, too. They're probably whispering right now as you read this. Maybe they sound like:

- "You're not strong enough to change this."
- "People like you don't get to have better."
- "You've tried before and failed, What makes you think this time will be different?"
- "Everyone will judge you if you leave."
- "You're being dramatic. It's not that bad."
- "You should be grateful for what you have."

These voices feel like wisdom, but they're just fear wearing a disguise. They're the old programming trying to keep you small; trying to convince you that the cage you know is better than the freedom you can't yet see.

How Patterns Live in Your Body

Patterns don't remain exclusively in your mind. They invade your body.

Growing up in chaos taught my nervous system to stay on high alert. I learned to read rooms like a survival skill. Fight or flight.

Walk into any space and immediately scan:

- Who's angry?
- Who needs something?
- What's the emotional temperature?
- How do I need to adjust myself to keep things calm?

My shoulders were permanently tense. My breathing stayed shallow. My stomach churned with anxiety I didn't even recognize as anxiety because it was so constant it felt normal.

When you grow up waiting for the next blow-up, your body learns to live on edge. Your nervous system gets stuck in fight-or-flight mode. You develop what researchers call hypervigilance—constantly scanning for threats, even when you're safe.

This shows up differently for everyone. Maybe your jaw clenches when conflict arises. Maybe your chest tightens when someone asks what you need. Maybe you hold your breath without realizing it. Maybe you can't sit still because stillness feels dangerous.

Your body keeps the score of every pattern you've ever lived. It remembers every time you made yourself small, every time you swallowed your truth, every time you chose someone else's comfort over your own safety.

If your body can learn patterns of surviving, it can also learn patterns of thriving.

The Common Thread

When I look back at my drinking, my marriage, my people-pleasing, my constant need for validation, there's one thread weaving through it all: I just didn't love myself.

That's the truth I had to face. I kept searching for someone else to fill that void. Whether it was alcohol numbing the pain, a man making me feel chosen, or applause for being "the talented one," I was always trying to earn my place in the room. Always performing. Always proving.

Deep down, all I ever wanted was to be loved and not feel like second best. I've always felt like chopped liver. The inner kid in me was screaming for a hug. But when you don't love yourself first, people can't mirror back what you're missing. They only reflect the cracks you already carry.

That was the thread weaving through it all. My drinking, my marriage, the vicious cycles of which I couldn't see my way out of. It wasn't that I was weak. I was empty in the place love was supposed to live. That emptiness disguised itself as strength. Being the peacemaker. Being the overachiever. Being the one who "had it together." But underneath it was the same old pattern: trying to hold onto scraps of love because I didn't believe I deserved the whole thing.

When Childhood Armor Becomes An Adult Prison

My patterns might look different from yours, but the underlying mechanics are the same. We all develop strategies for getting our needs met when direct asking feels too risky.

Some of us become the Achiever—working ourselves to death trying to earn love through accomplishment.

Some become the Invisible One—making ourselves so small and easy that no one has a reason to leave.

Some become the Fixer—making ourselves indispensable by solving everyone else's problems.

Some become the Rebel—pushing everyone away before they can reject us.

Some become the Victim—getting attention through suffering because it's the only attention that feels safe.

Some become the Performer—entertaining everyone so they'll want us around.

Maybe you're the Provider—working yourself into the ground because your worth equals your paycheck.

Maybe you're the Stoic—swallowing every emotion because vulnerability equals weakness.

Maybe you're the Protector—taking on everyone's problems because being needed feels like being loved.

None of these strategies are wrong. They all made perfect sense when we developed them. A five-year-old who learns that making people laugh keeps the peace is simply doing what they need to survive. A child who becomes the helper—always cleaning up, always fixing—might believe that being useful is the only way to earn love. A teenager who shrinks into the background to avoid conflict is adapting to their environment. Another might go the opposite way—loud, rebellious, always in motion—because attention, even the negative kind, feels safer than being forgotten.

The point is, every one of these responses is intelligence in action. They're protective strategies wired into us long before we realize we have a choice. They get us through the moment, even if they cost us later on.

Whether you're a man who learned to suppress emotions to appear strong, or a woman who learned to suppress needs to appear easy-going, the mechanics are the same. We all develop strategies to get our needs met when being direct feels too dangerous.

But strategies that save us as children can suffocate us as adults. The same patterns that once protected us can become the very things that keep us from the life we actually want.

The unspoken rule I carried everywhere was simple: Keep your head down, don't cause problems, don't make things harder than they already are.

I followed that rule for decades. It made me docile when I should have been fierce. Quiet when I should have been loud. Scared to reach for more when I had every right to want everything.

Statistical studies have found that children from alcoholic homes are significantly more likely to develop anxiety disorders, depression, and relationship difficulties.

We're also more likely to become people-pleasers, overachievers, and caretakers. The survival skills that got us through childhood often become the very patterns that limit us in adulthood.

Then around June 2023, something snapped. I stepped into my "can't nobody tell me nothing" era. By then, I'd gotten to know myself so well that there was no going back. I knew what I was capable of.

I realized I had it in me to flip the board, but then I questioned that. If I could flip the board, why not start a new game? Forget your table. Forget your game. Let me show you how to do it.

The Truth They Won't Tell You

You're not broken. You're just programmed.

Every pattern that's killing you slowly made perfect sense once upon a time. Does the people-pleasing exhaust you now? It kept you safe as a kid. Does the overgiving leave you empty? It was how you earned love when love came with conditions. How about the constant need to prove your worth? It was survival when being "too much" meant being rejected.

Your patterns aren't character flaws. They're outdated software running programs that no longer serve the life you're trying to build.

I spent years thinking I was destined to repeat the same cycles forever. What I didn't realize was that I already had a secret superpower: I could see patterns clearly. Even in the middle of the mess, I noticed the same loops showing up over and over. I just didn't know I had the ability to rewrite them yet.

That recognition felt like confirmation of how stuck I was. Only later did I understand it was actually proof of my capability.

The first pattern I ever truly broke was drinking. For so long, alcohol had been my comfort, my best friend who saw me through everything, my way of shutting down the noise in my head. Every morning after, the shame and pain were heavier. I hit that point where I couldn't keep doing it mentally, way before my body started shutting down physically.

I didn't call it "redesigning a pattern" then. I just knew I had to survive. Looking back now, I can see what really happened. That moment was me choosing something different, even when it scared me. Even when it physically hurt because withdrawals aren't pretty.

That was the first time I broke a pattern on purpose. The first glimpse of the truth I see so clearly now: I wasn't doomed to keep repeating. I had the power to rewire everything.

I learned mindfulness. The more I showed up with consistency and discipline, the more I proved to myself that change was possible. That's when I realized I could actually move the needle— not by trying to change everything at once, but by focusing on one goal at a time.

The Pattern Maker Awakens

Patterns trick you into thinking you're powerless when you're actually the one running the show.

For years, I thought I was the victim of my circumstances. The daughter of an alcoholic. The product of generational trauma. The woman who couldn't stop choosing the wrong people. I was all those things, but I was something else, too.

I was the Pattern Maker.

Not the victim of my patterns, but the architect of my own redesign. Every time I'd rebuilt myself before, I'd move through the same phases without realizing it. Growth, Love, Overcome, Wisdom. I'd been living the solution long before I gave it a name.

The moment I realized this, everything shifted. I stopped asking, "Why does this keep happening to me?" and started asking, "What pattern am I running here, and how do I want to change it?"

That question changed my life. And it's about to change yours, too.

Questions for Your Own Pattern Recognition:

1. Where do you feel patterns living in your body? What happens to your breathing when conflict arises? How do your shoulders respond to stress?
2. What would your patterns say to keep you trapped?

What lies do they whisper when you think about changing?

3. What's the common thread running through your relationships, your work, your self-talk? What are you always trying to earn or prove or avoid?
4. What rule that you didn't make has been running your life? How long have you been following it?

The Road Ahead

Because if you picked up this book, you're already further along than you think. You're already starting to see the patterns. You're already questioning the familiar. You're already reaching for something different.

You're the Pattern Maker. You just forgot for a while.

Time to remember.

The next step isn't to judge yourself for the patterns you've been running. It's to understand why they made sense when you created them, and then decide if they still serve who you're becoming.

In the next chapter, we're going to talk about the myth of holding it all together—that performance you've been putting on while your world crumbles behind the scenes. Because here's the thing: recognizing the patterns is just the beginning. Now we need to understand why you've been working so hard to make them look good.

Chapter 2:
The Myth of Having It All Together

Hair done. Makeup on. Smile ready.

Every morning, I'd step into character like an actress preparing for the performance of her life. The bathroom mirror became my backstage, where I'd change from the woman who barely slept into the woman who had it all together.

The routine was flawless. Foundation to cover the exhaustion etched under my eyes. Concealer for the stress breakouts. Mascara to make my eyes look alive when everything inside felt dead. I'd stand there, painting over the evidence of my slow collapse, creating the masterpiece everyone expected to see.

"You look great today," colleagues would say as I walked through the squadron. They had no idea what they were applauding.

I was dying in slow motion, and I'd become a master at making it look like living.

Behind the polished exterior, my marriage was falling apart. I was drinking in secret. Not social drinking, but strategic drinking designed to get me intoxicated as quickly as possible. I'd developed a whole system for hiding it, going from store to store in my neighborhood so no single cashier could track how much I consumed each day. Each transaction was calculated, each purchase planned. I was running a covert operation against my own life.

My body was failing me in ways that should have shocked me into making a change. Lab work showed my kidneys were failing, the numbers inching me closer to my own death with each test. I wasn't hydrating. My food intake was terrible. I was surviving on caffeine, adrenaline, and the bare minimum required to keep the show going.

Nobody had a clue because I made sure they didn't.

I was what experts call a "high-functioning alcoholic," that contradictory creature who can maintain jobs and relationships while slowly self-destructing. Research shows that functional alcoholics account for nearly 20% of all alcoholics in the United States. We're middle-aged, well-educated professionals with “reliable” jobs and families. We're the ones who don't fit the stereotype, which makes us nearly impossible to detect.

I hated looking stupid, so I got excellent at keeping secrets. Every morning, I'd count down the minutes until I could be alone again, until the curtain could drop and I could stop performing with strength I didn't feel.

This wasn't my story alone. Millions of women have learned to excel at appearing okay while falling apart behind closed doors. We're the overachievers, the problem-solvers, the ones everyone depends on. We're dying under the weight of our own performance.

Studies reveal that 88% of high-achieving individuals report at least moderate feelings of what psychologists call the "imposter phenomenon." This persistent fear of being exposed as a fraud exists despite evidence of competence and success. The research on women and alcohol tells an increasingly troubling story. Women are experiencing alcohol-related problems sooner and at lower drinking amounts than men. We're more likely to hide our drinking, more likely to drink alone, and more likely to use alcohol as an emotional regulation rather than a social connection.

I wasn't drinking because I was weak. I was drinking because I was performing at an unsustainable level, and alcohol was the only thing that could quiet the noise long enough for me to catch my breath.

Every "How are you doing?" demanded an Oscar-worthy response: "Great! Busy, but great. You know how it is." And they did know how it was, because they were performing their own version of the same lie.

The military had trained me well for this kind of performance. "Hold your bearing," they taught us. "Follow orders. Get the job done. The mission comes first." That training served me in many ways. It built resilience, discipline, the ability to push through when most people would quit. But it also trained me to hide in plain sight, to stand tall and look grounded while quietly locking away anything that might be read as weakness.

The production demanded everything from me. By the time I got off shift, I was completely drained from holding it all together. The second that door closed behind me, I'd crumble. I wasn't strong—I was petrified of what would happen if I stopped performing.

That's when the drinking would begin. Systematic numbing designed to silence the voice inside my head that kept whispering the reality I couldn't bear to hear. This life is killing you, and everyone thinks you're handling it beautifully.

The "Fine"dentity Trap

Being "fine" wasn't just something I said. It became who I was.

The military made "fine" a default setting, but somewhere along the way, it morphed into my entire identity. Fine became my brand. My reputation. My survival mechanism.

The "fine"dentity trap is insidious because it feels like strength. When everyone around you is falling apart and you're the one holding it together, you start to believe that's your purpose. Your value. Your worth as a human being gets tied to your ability to appear calm and collected.

Recent studies suggest that female enlisted service members face significantly higher rates of stress, anxiety, and depression compared to their male counterparts, often stemming from the unique pressures of military culture and the expectation to maintain composure under extreme conditions. Female veterans are 2.53 times more likely to develop PTSD than their male counterparts, yet they're also more likely to hide their struggles and avoid seeking help.

As enlisted personnel, we're trained to follow orders, stay mission-ready, and never show weakness. We become so invested in the "fine" identity that admitting otherwise feels like admitting failure—not just personal failure, but failure to the mission, to our unit, to the uniform we wear.

The day I knew my "strength" was really survival was the day I couldn't switch it off. I could power through meetings, conversations, and family dinners. But the second that door closed behind me, I'd crumble.

I wasn't strong. I was scared of what would happen if I stopped being fine.

The "fine"dentity had become so automatic that I'd forgotten it was a choice. Being fine wasn't what I did anymore. It was who I was. I'd built my entire sense of self around being okay. Being the fierce one. The take-no-nonsense one. The "we don't show weakness around here" one. If I wasn't the woman who had it all together, I didn't know who I was.

The "fine"dentity demands constant maintenance. Every interaction had to be managed. Every response had to be calculated. Every emotion had to be filtered through the question: "Will this threaten my fine identity?" The exhaustion was relentless, but the alternative felt like death. If I wasn't fine, then what was I?

The trap wasn't built overnight. It took years of reinforcement, years of being rewarded for appearing strong while my actual needs went unmet. Every time someone said, "I don't know how you do it," or "You're so strong," they were feeding my "fine"dentity. The compliments validated the performance, making me believe that my worth was tied to my ability to appear unshakable.

But an identity built on fine is fundamentally unstable because fine is a lie.

I was spending more energy protecting my "fine"dentity than I was trying to actually get okay. Maintaining the image took more out of me than my actual problems. The identity had become more exhausting than the pain it was meant to hide.

The cost was complete isolation. I couldn't let anyone see the cracks because that would destroy the "fine" person I'd convinced everyone I was. Nobody could help me because helping would require admitting I wasn't actually fine.

When people did try to check in, I'd deflect with military precision. "Just tired," I'd say. "It's been a long week." These weren't lies exactly, but they were identity protection. The whole truth was that the woman who was always fine was drowning in plain sight.

The scariest part wasn't that I was falling apart. The scariest part was that I was falling apart while everyone around me thought I was the woman who never fell apart. My "fine"dentity had become my prison.

Breaking free meant grieving the "fine" woman everyone knew. It meant accepting that I'd built my entire sense of self on a performance. It meant rebuilding my entire identity from the ground up.

Now I understand that real identity comes from authenticity, not performance. The "fine"dentity taught me to endure. Authentic identity taught me to heal. The difference between the two changed everything.

Dangerous Validation

Most people will buy your fake-self completely.

Friends, coworkers, extended family never questioned the act. I was so consistent with my performance that they never had reason to doubt it. When you show up every day with your hair done, your smile ready, your responsibilities handled, people assume you're handling everything else too.

The success of my deception became its own trap. Every "You're so strong" comment fed my addiction to the performance. Every "I don't know how you do it" validated my choice to keep the mask welded on. The compliments weren't just nice to hear. They were proof that my strategy was working, that I was successfully protecting everyone from the truth of who I was becoming.

Research shows that high-functioning individuals in crisis are particularly difficult to detect because their coping mechanisms look like strength. Unlike someone whose life is visibly falling apart, functional addicts and high-achievers in breakdown maintain their external responsibilities. We pay our bills, show up to work, remember birthdays, keep our houses clean. The performance is so convincing that we even start to believe it sometimes.

My mom and sister saw through it, though.

They knew the pain because they had their own, so they recognized the symptoms. When you've lived in your own version of hell, you develop radar for other people's suffering, even when they're trying to hide it. I'd give them just enough truth to satisfy their concern without letting them close enough to see the whole picture.

The fact that almost everyone believed me made me double down on the act. But the ones who didn't believe it, like my mom and sister, horrified me. If they could tell, maybe others could too. So instead of taking their concern as an invitation to get help, I pulled the mask on even tighter.

This is the insidious cycle of high-functioning breakdown. The better you get at hiding it, the more isolated you become. The more isolated you become, the more you need to hide it. Your competence becomes your camouflage, and your achievements become your armor.

The people who loved me most were simultaneously my biggest threat and my greatest hope. They saw through the performance because they cared enough to look past the surface. But their seeing felt dangerous because it threatened the identity I'd built my entire sense of safety around.

I surrounded myself with believers because believers were safer than seers. Believers took me at face value. Believers didn't ask hard questions. Believers didn't threaten my carefully constructed reality.

But believers also couldn't help me. And deep down, I knew that.

If you recognize yourself in this story, look around at your own audience. Who are your believers, and who are your seers?

The believers will applaud your performance and tell you how strong you are. The seers will ask if you're really okay, even when you insist you are.

The believers feel safer, but the seers are the ones who might actually save your life.

What We're Really Hiding From

If I'd told the truth about how shattered I really was, I was scared people would see me differently. Not just judge me, but worse than that. Treat me like I was broken.

The fear wasn't really about criticism. I could handle criticism. The terror was about losing my autonomy, my credibility, my place in the world I'd worked so hard to build.

I didn't want pity. I wasn't about to become someone's project. The thought of people looking at me with concern instead of respect, of offering help instead of asking for it, felt like a form of death.

My word was my bond, and I worried that if people saw me at my lowest, they'd question everything I'd ever said or done. Like my entire track record would be invalidated by my current struggle. This is the all-or-nothing thinking that traps high-achievers. We believe that admitting any weakness erases all our strength.

Research on perfectionism shows that people like me often tie their worth to their ability to appear flawless. We're not afraid of being human. We're afraid of being seen as frauds who were never as capable as we pretended to be. The imposter syndrome runs so deep that we genuinely believe our struggles would expose us as liars rather than reveal us as human.

I was deathly afraid that my integrity would be questioned. That people would think, "If she's this much of a mess, how can we trust anything she says?" The logical mind knows this isn't how relationships work, but the fear brain doesn't deal in logic.

The competence trap is real. When your value to others is based on your ability to handle everything, admitting you can't handle something feels like admitting you're worthless. I'd spent so many years being everyone's reliable person that I didn't know how to exist any other way.

What I feared most was losing respect. Not the surface-level respect that comes from being polite, but the deep respect that comes from being seen as capable. I thought if people knew how bad it really was, they'd lose faith in my judgment, my character, my fundamental worth as a human being.

The truth is, I was already broken. The performance wasn't hiding my brokenness. It was breaking me further every day. But admitting that felt impossible because I'd confused being strong with never needing help.

Behind every "I'm okay" is a person scared stiff of being seen as anything else. We're not lying to hurt people. We're lying to protect ourselves from a rejection we're sure is coming if anyone sees who we really are behind the performance.

The irony is that the people who truly love us want to know who we really are. They want to help us carry the weight. But we're so afraid of being a burden that we become one anyway, just in a different way. We burden people with our performance, our distance, our refusal to let them in.

Breaking free from this terror requires understanding that being human isn't a character flaw. Struggling doesn't invalidate your strength. Needing help doesn't make you weak.

But when you're trapped in fear, none of that feels true. It all feels like excuses for being the failure you've always been afraid you were.

The Smoke Bomb Strategy

We use humor like a smoke bomb. Smoke and mirrors. Throw out a funny comment, get everyone laughing, and slip away from the conversation before anyone gets close to anything true.

Humor became my most sophisticated deflection tool. Not the kind of humor that connects people, but the kind that creates distance while appearing to do the opposite. I'd wave something thought-provoking and happy in people's faces, uplift the room, and then retire to the hell I'd made for myself.

The strategy was flawless. Someone would ask how I was really doing, and I'd crack a joke about being too busy to fall apart or too stubborn to quit. Everyone would laugh, the tension would dissolve, and I'd successfully avoided having to answer the question honestly.

Being funny became another performance within the performance. I was pretending to be entertaining while I was pretending to have it together. It was exhausting, but it worked.

Research shows that humor is one of the most common defense mechanisms among high-functioning people in crisis. Unlike other deflection strategies, humor actually makes people feel good, so they're less likely to push back against it. When someone makes you laugh, you don't usually follow up with harder questions.

The problem with using humor as armor is that it becomes another identity you have to maintain. Now you're not just the strong one, you're also the funny one. People start expecting entertainment from you. They come to you for laughs when you barely have energy to breathe.

I became addicted to making other people feel good because it was the only way I could feel valuable. If I couldn't be happy, at least I could make everyone else happy. If I couldn't fix my own problems, at least I could lighten everyone else's mood.

The loneliness of being everyone's entertainer while never being entertained yourself is profound. You spend so much energy making other people laugh that you forget what genuine joy feels like. You become a happiness dealer who never uses their own product.

Comedy became crisis management. Every family dinner, every work meeting, every social gathering became an opportunity to perform my way out of deeper connection. I'd rather have people think I was hilariously overwhelmed than actually overwhelmed.

The smoke bomb strategy worked so well that I started using it on myself. Instead of sitting with my pain, I'd joke about it. Instead of processing my trauma, I'd make it into material. Humor wasn't helping me heal. It was helping me avoid the very feelings that needed to be felt.

If you find yourself deflecting every serious conversation with a joke, if people always comment on how funny you are but you feel empty inside, if you can't be serious without feeling deeply uncomfortable, you might be using humor as armor, too.

There's a difference between using humor to cope and using humor to hide. Coping humor helps you process difficult emotions. Hiding humor helps you avoid them entirely.

The day I stopped being everyone's comedian was the day I started being my own friend.

It Can't "Wait Until Tomorrow"

If you've been saying "things will get better when..." for more than a few weeks, you're not dealing with a rough patch anymore. You're dealing with a pattern. If you've been postponing your own well-being for years, waiting for the right time to address your problems, that waiting has become the problem.

Research shows that the difference between acute stress and chronic dysfunction is duration. Acute stress motivates action. Chronic stress creates adaptation. When you adapt to dysfunction long enough, dysfunction starts to feel normal.

It all started after I left Korea in January 2017. That year at Camp Humphreys was one of the hardest of my life. The weight of that short tour still lingers—I carry it with me in ways I never expected. A portion of my VA disability compensation today is tied to PTSD from military sexual trauma that happened during that time. It marked me. It changed the way I moved through the world.

In the middle of 2016, my ex-husband and I hit a breaking point. We both knew our marriage was finished. There was no more pretending, no more trying to glue the pieces back together. We went to see the military legal team at Osan Air Base, ready to make it official. I remember walking into that office with the kind of heavy silence between us that says everything without a word.

But when we learned it would cost $3,000 to divorce in Korea—and only $300 if we waited until we got back to the States—we hesitated.

We didn't have the extra money, so we decided to wait. Bad idea.

Instead of ending it then, we slipped right back into the loop with each other. What should have been closure became another delay. And that delay stretched into another eight years. We dragged it out until our 14-month divorce finally wrapped in February 2025.

In the end, that $2,700 "savings" cost me almost ten years of my life.

When I came back to the States in January 2017, the weight of it all hit me. I spiraled into deep depression. By 2018, I felt suicidal. Between December 2017 and January 2019, my weight shot from 165 pounds to 295 pounds during my pregnancy with my oldest daughter.

I started hiding. Baggy clothes, canceled plans, avoiding anything I used to love because I didn't want the reminder of what I'd lost. I told myself I'd "get back on track" when I had more energy, but the energy never came.

In May 2018, I was honorably discharged from the Air Force after six years as a weather forecaster. I thought getting out would bring me peace, but without the structure, the depression hit harder. Every day I stayed in that same merciless cycle, it felt like another piece of me went missing.

Here's how to tell if you're in a slow collapse rather than a rough patch: Rough patches have clear beginning and ending points. Slow collapses feel eternal. Rough patches motivate you to make changes. Slow collapses make change feel impossible.

If you're reading this and recognizing yourself, the most important thing to understand is that slow collapse isn't a character flaw. It's what happens when you've been strong for so long that you don't remember how to ask for help. It's what happens when you've been managing everyone else's problems while your own problems manage you.

Chapter 3:
Rock Bottom Lessons

I was curled on the shower floor with my knees pulled to my chest, fists jammed shut. No matter how hard I tried, I couldn't open them. My hands shook so violently that my nails left crescent cuts in my palms.

A few feet away, my daughter sat in the tub, the tablet balanced on a little stool beside the tub while she sat watching from the side. Cartoons played on the screen as she giggled at something I couldn't hear. The sound of her laugh bounced off the bathroom walls. She was fine. I was not.

My chest hammered, each beat so loud I swore the neighbors could hear it. My stomach lurched, but nothing came out except the sour burn of acid. I was gasping like a fish on concrete, desperate for air that wouldn't come. The harder I fought for a deep breath, the more my body refused.

There is nothing glamorous about panic. No slow-motion breakdown, no poetic collapse. Only sweat, bile, and the kind of terror that makes time melt into oblivion. Seconds feel like hours. Minutes feel like decades.

I was crumpled on the shower floor, skin slick with water, breath sour with alcohol. Droplets hit my shoulders as the spray kept running. For a split second, I thought it might be a heart attack. Some part of me almost wished it was. At least then there'd be an explanation.

But this was worse. This was not random. This was the inevitable bill. Every drink I had poured. Every secret I had buried. Every night I whispered, "Tomorrow I'll quit." All of it landed here. On the floor. Next to my child.

I had been here before. The shakes, the racing heart. The clenched fists were new, though. A new symptom in a body that was finally done carrying me through my own denial.

Leilani laughed again. She slapped her small hands against the water, splashing the rim of the tub. The droplets hit my skin and burned like acid. Her joy and my collapse coexisted in the same air, and the contrast sliced me in half. Her life was just beginning. Mine was hanging by a thread.

People imagine rock bottom as a dramatic event. Sirens. ER visits. Blue lights flashing in the rearview. The reality is quieter. Rock bottom shows up in ordinary places—the shower you have cleaned a hundred times, the bathroom with its stack of folded towels—until you realize the life you have been faking cannot stretch another inch.

I lay there listening to her laughter and my own ragged breaths, and for the first time, I admitted the thought I had been running from: I was dying in slow motion.

And if something didn't change, it was going to take us both down.

Functional vs. Absolute Rock Bottom

For years, I told myself I hadn't hit rock bottom because I was still functioning. I still got up for work. I still put makeup on. I still laughed at the right moments and hit deadlines. From the outside, I looked stable enough to pass.

That was the problem. A functional rock bottom wears a mask. It gives you precisely enough evidence to argue with yourself. You can point to the paycheck, the clean house, the birthday parties, and say, "See? I'm fine."

Functional rock bottom is a slow death. You can keep the plates spinning, but every day you lose a little more of yourself. For me, it looked like hiding empty bottles in the back of cabinets, stashing cans in the closet, always keeping two on hand in case one wasn't enough. I could still parent, still smile, still joke at the squadron. But the scaffolding was rotting.

Absolute rock bottom stripped all of that away. My body refused to play along. Panic attacks dropped me to the floor. My hands seized. My heart raced like it was trying to leave my chest. I woke palpitating from withdrawals, convinced I was dying in my sleep. Even the bathroom mirror stopped lying. The bloodshot eyes, the gray skin, the way my face sagged with exhaustion. It was no longer possible to hide, not even from myself.

That space between the two is the most dangerous place you can live. It lets you bargain. You think you are not "bad enough" to quit, not desperate enough to change. You tell yourself that if you can keep going to work, keep paying bills, keep smiling for photos, then you are not like those people who have truly fallen apart.

Addiction thrives in that middle ground. It lets you believe you are both fine and failing at the same time. It's like watering a plant that has already died. You keep pouring in energy, hoping something will come back to life, while deep down you know it won't.

Clinicians have a name for that in-between stage you've probably heard before: Denial. It's the mind's way of buying time, patching the cracks with excuses. Research shows that nearly half of the people who meet the criteria for alcohol dependence delay seeking help for more than eight years.

Eight years of bargaining. Eight years of false starts. Eight years of waking up certain you'll quit tomorrow.

That was me. Functioning on paper, unraveling in private. Mornings began with shaky hands and the sour weight of regret. Evenings ended with the bottle waiting like a ritual I never dared to break. I didn't call it addiction. I called it "taking the edge off." I folded it into my schedule the same way someone else folds laundry. Routine. Ordinary.

Absolute rock bottom doesn't play tricks. It rips the mask away. Hands trembling so hard I couldn't hold a pen. Nights where I crawled across the floor, too anxious to sleep, too weak to stand.

Withdrawals don't whisper. They howl.

The Illusion of Control

I told myself I wasn't like "those people." The ones slurring in parking lots, the ones with court dates, the ones losing custody. I still paid my bills. I still got dressed in clean clothes. I still kissed my daughter goodnight.

That was the trick. I clung to every scrap of evidence that said I was still in control. If I kept the house spotless, then I wasn't really falling apart. If I made it to work, then I wasn't really an addict. If I smiled in the group photo, then no one could see the truth.

Denial thrives on comparison. As long as I could find someone "worse," I could convince myself I wasn't that bad. Psychologists call it the illusion of control. It's when you confuse survival with stability, mistaking functioning for thriving.

But the truth was, alcohol had the reins. I didn't decide when to drink. It decided when I would start shaking. I didn't decide when to stop. It decided when the bottle ran out.

I was never in control. I was the one being managed, measured, rationed. And as long as I believed the lie, I stayed stuck in the middle ground where nothing changed.

Alcohol billed me in installments, and the receipts were everywhere.

It stole my money first. Two bottles here, a six-pack there, slipped into grocery runs so no one would notice. I never added it up, but if you multiplied those purchases across years, you'd have tuition for college, a down payment on a home. Instead, I bought blackouts.

It stole my time. Entire mornings spent in bed with headaches. Afternoons wasted calculating when and how to sneak the next drink. Hours I could have spent reading to my daughter or walking outside vanished in service to the bottle.

It stole my body. Enamel ground down until my dentist warned me. A stomach lining eaten raw. Nights drenched in sweat. A body twenty years older than it should have been.

But the worst bill came in love. Every hidden can, every excuse, every fake smile widened the gap between me and the people I swore I loved. Trust drained. Connection drained.

National reports estimate alcohol costs the U.S. nearly $249 billion annually when you count health care, productivity, and accidents. But the numbers don't mean anything until you're the one paying with your life. For me, it was more than a statistic. It was bankruptcy of the soul.

The Military Mask

Discipline had been drilled into me. Wake up. Uniform. Mission. Repeat. That rhythm had once been my lifeline. It gave me something to hold onto when I felt like I was falling apart.

But the same discipline also became my mask. It made me good at functioning while broken. Good at hiding the mess. Good at showing up to do the job while my world burned inside.

The Air Force had trained me to push through, to never complain, to never show weakness. That looked like strength, but it was survival. And survival at all costs meant I carried habits that no longer served me. What worked in uniform was suffocating me as a civilian.

At some point, the structure turned into a cage. I realized I would have to unlearn parts of that training and redefine strength on my own terms. Strength was no longer about holding the line. It was about laying one down and saying, "I will not cross this again."

For the first time, I saw my own obsessive nature not as a curse but as a battle-tested blessing. I had poured it into alcohol, into chaos, into anything that could quiet the noise. But if I could turn that same energy toward building instead of destroying, it could be the very thing that rebuilt me.

Psychologists have long recognized this paradox. The same traits that drive compulsive behavior—focus, intensity, persistence—can be redirected into resilience and growth when paired with intention. Addiction wasn't my weakness. It was untamed power waiting for a new outlet.

Grieving the Old Identity

I didn't only grieve the alcohol. I grieved the version of me who needed it.

The girl who believed she couldn't walk into a room without a drink in her hand. The woman who wore toughness like armor and laughed louder than her pain. The one who felt she belonged only if she could keep up with the chaos.

Letting go of her was like cutting off air, because for years, she was my survival. I also grieved the chaos itself. The late nights. The hangovers. The predictable rhythm of destruction. As toxic as it was, it felt safer than the silence I would face without it.

I even grieved the lies. Lies that whispered addiction was in my DNA, that I was doomed, that freedom was for other people. Lies that became my twisted comfort blanket.

When I buried those identities, I buried the illusion that I had to earn my place in the world. I buried the belief that silence was weakness. In that grief, I uncovered a truth: I wasn't unfixable. I wasn't broken. My obsessive energy wasn't my enemy. It was my power source. Once I flipped it, I got hooked on healing. Addicted to growth. Obsessed with becoming and living whole.

When I left the Air Force in 2018, I thought life would fall into place. Instead, it felt like freefall.

I took a cashier job at Walmart to keep busy, every beep of the scanner reminding me how far I had fallen from the sense of purpose I once had. I enrolled in classes, piled up credits, and never finished. No degree. No follow-through. I told myself success belonged to people with more discipline, more brains, more worth.

Then came motherhood. My daughter was born in January 2019, and I stayed home while my ex paid the bills. From the outside, I did everything "right." Meals cooked. House spotless. Baby cared for. Inside, I was unraveling.

I had postpartum depression layered on top of alcoholism. I could give her everything and still believe I wasn't enough. I could outperform every mom I knew and still feel like a failure. That guilt poured straight into the bottle.

The bottle became a ritual. It steadied the shakes, quieted the noise, gave me false strength. But the same ritual that promised relief was choking me tighter every day.

I sometimes think of it as a funeral. Not with flowers or hymns. A private burial for the woman I had been.

Here lies the girl who needed a drink to feel liked.
Here lies the woman who could outdrink any man, who mistook toughness for belonging.
Here lies the one who thought chaos was safer than silence.

I cried for her. I mourned her. She was my survival for so long that letting her go felt like suffocating. But survival isn't the same as living. She couldn't build the life I wanted. She couldn't raise my daughter into something better. She had to die so I could live.

The grief was real. But so was the relief. I didn't just bury the bottle. I buried the belief that I had to earn love. I buried the lie that silence meant strength.

That funeral gave me back myself.

The Bargaining Cycle

Morning: Today's the day. I can't do this anymore. My body hurts. My head won't stop pounding. Today I quit.

Midday: Maybe one. One to take the edge off. Nobody has to know.

Evening: One wasn't enough. I'll stop after this next one. I just need to feel normal before bed.

Night: Tomorrow. Tomorrow I'll quit for real.

That was the cycle. Over and over. Like a broken record that never skipped. No poetry. No clever metaphor. Just endless bargaining until I was too drunk to care and too numb to fight.

Clinicians call this "the relapse loop." It is one of the most common experiences for people with substance dependence—a cycle of intention, justification, relapse, and shame. Studies show most people attempt to quit multiple times before long-term recovery takes hold. I was no exception.

At first, rock bottom felt like humiliation. Proof I was too far gone. Proof I had become everything I swore I would never be.

But in the middle of that shame, I noticed something small. I was still breathing. My chest still rose and fell, even if the breaths were shallow. My daughter was still there, her laugh breaking through the fog like sunlight I didn't deserve.

Life hadn't abandoned me, even when I abandoned myself.

That flicker cracked something open. It showed me possibilities. Maybe rock bottom wasn't proof I was broken. Maybe it was proof I had run out of places to hide.

Because down there, stripped of every excuse, every mask, every bottle, there was nowhere left to run.

Rock bottom didn't kill me. It revealed I could survive without the crutch I thought I needed. It taught me silence wasn't empty. Silence was space. In that space, under years of noise, I found a fragile seed of hope. Alive. Waiting.

That was the shift. From shame to possibility. From "I'll never be free" to "What if I could?" Rock bottom wasn't the end. It was the floor I pushed off from.

Checkpoint

If you are here, I want you to hear me: collapse is not the end. It might be the moment you stop hiding.

Ask yourself:

- Where are you bargaining with yourself the way I did?
- What masks are you still wearing to look "functional"?
- What part of you needs to be buried so you can be reborn?

You don't have to answer out loud. Even admitting the question is a start. Rock bottom can be the end of denial and the beginning of possibility.

PART TWO:
THE GLOW METHOD — THE INSIDE-OUT PATH

Before You Read Part Two

You've made it through the dark night of your soul in Part One. You've seen the patterns, felt the pain, and maybe even recognized yourself in some of those rock-bottom moments. That was the diagnosis. This is the prescription.

You can read Part Two while you're curled up on the couch with a cup of coffee, but you won't get the most out of it.

This section is your workbook. Your manual. Your step-by-step guide to breaking the patterns that have been running your life and building new ones that actually serve you.

The chapters ahead will look different from what you just read.

While Part One was about understanding your patterns, Part Two is about changing them. While Part One was about recognition, Part Two is about action. This is where the real work begins.

Knowledge Without Action Is Just Entertainment

You can read every self-help book ever written, memorize every quote about change, and understand exactly what's wrong with your life. But if you don't apply what you learn, nothing changes. Knowledge without action is just expensive entertainment.

The people who transform their lives aren't necessarily the smartest or the most motivated. They're the ones who take what they learn and actually use it. They're the ones who do the exercises instead of just reading them. They're the ones who treat their healing like the mission-critical work it is.

Applied knowledge is power. But only when it's used in the right way, at the right time, with the right commitment to follow through.

This Is Your Transformation Manual

In the next four chapters, you'll learn the GLOW Method—the same framework I used to rebuild my life from the ground up:

G - Growth: How to own your beginning and stop waiting for perfect conditions to change your life

L - Love: How to stop breaking your own heart and start treating yourself like someone worth fighting for

O - Overcome: How to break old patterns and heal what's been stored in your body for years

W - Wisdom: How to turn your pain into purpose and design a life from which you don't want to escape

Each chapter contains real stories from my journey, research-backed strategies, and most importantly—action steps that work. Not theory. Not concepts. Actual tools you can use today to start changing your life.

How to Use This Section for Maximum Impact

This isn't a book to race through. It's a manual to work through. Here's how to get the most out of every chapter:

Read in Bite-Sized Chunks: Don't try to consume an entire chapter in one sitting. Read one section at a time, then stop and let it sink in. Your brain needs time to process new information before it can integrate it.

Actually Do the Action Steps: Each chapter contains multiple action steps designed to help you apply what you're learning immediately. These aren't optional. They're the difference between reading about change and actually changing. Set aside 5–10 minutes to complete each mini-exercise as you encounter it.

Honor the Checkpoints: At the end of each chapter, you'll find comprehensive exercises that tie everything together. Block out 20-30 minutes to complete these thoroughly. Don't skip them. Don't save them for later. Do them while the material is fresh in your mind.

Make This Book Yours: Grab a pen. Scribble in the margins. Highlight what resonates. Circle what challenges you. Write angry responses to things that trigger you. This book should look well-used by the time you're done with it, because that means you actually used it.

Track Your Progress: Notice what shifts as you work through each chapter. What gets easier? What stays difficult?

What surprises you? This awareness will help you understand your own patterns and celebrate your growth.

Be Patient With the Process: Transformation doesn't happen overnight. Some exercises will feel natural immediately. Others will feel impossible at first. That's normal. The things that feel hardest are often the things you need most. Trust the process even when you can't see immediate results.

The Work Is the Reward

This section will ask things of you that other books won't. It will require you to get uncomfortable, to look at yourself honestly, to try new approaches even when they feel foreign. It will ask you to stop being a passive consumer of information and start being an active participant in your own healing.

Some days you'll want to skip the exercises and just read the stories. Some days the action steps will feel too hard or too vulnerable. Some days you'll want to put the book down and go back to your familiar patterns.

Do the work anyway.

The exercises aren't busy work. They're not add-ons to make the book longer. They're the actual mechanism of change. They're how you take the insights from your mind and embed them in your body, your habits, your daily life.

The people who complete these exercises—really complete them, not just skim through them—are the ones who write to tell me their lives changed. They're the ones who break patterns that seem unbreakable. They're the ones who finally become the person they always knew they could be.

Your Transformation Starts Now

You've already survived everything that brought you to this point. You've already demonstrated more strength than you probably give yourself credit for. Now it's time to use that strength intentionally, to direct it toward building the life you actually want instead of just surviving the life you have.

The GLOW Method isn't magic. It's not a quick fix. It's a proven system for creating lasting change from the inside out. But it only works if you work it.

So grab that pen. Clear some space on your calendar. Turn off the distractions. This is your time to stop merely *reading* about change and start *creating* it.

Your transformation is waiting on the other side of your willingness to do the work.

Let's begin.

Chapter 4:
G – Growth – Owning Your Beginning

June 2021. I'm staring at the phone number I've been carrying around for three months.

Not because I was in a crisis. I'd survived that part. The shower floors, the loaded gun, the nights when my daughter's laugh was the only thing keeping me tethered to this world. All of that was behind me now.

This was different. This was the quiet space after the storm, when you're sitting in the wreckage, wondering what you're supposed to build with broken pieces.

I wasn't drowning anymore, but I wasn't swimming either. I was treading water in that dangerous middle space where you can survive indefinitely but never actually get anywhere. Familiar pain dressed up as stability.

The number belonged to the VA. I'd written it down after overhearing someone mention the substance abuse programs they offered. It planted a seed—that maybe I could go that route too. Whatever that meant. People who drank too much. People who came back from deployments different than they left. People whose military training had taught them how to function even while falling apart.

For ninety-three days, I carried that piece of paper in my wallet. Right behind my driver's license where I'd see it every time I opened it. A daily reminder of the choice I continued not making.

Every morning I'd wake up thinking, "Today I'll call." Then I'd find countless reasons why tomorrow would be better. I needed to be more prepared. I should figure out what to say first. Maybe I should wait until I feel stronger. Maybe I should try fixing it myself one more time.

Excuses. All of it.

The truth was, I was waiting to feel ready. And ready never comes when you're sitting still.

Ready is something you become by moving forward, not something you feel before you start.

One morning, I was making breakfast for Leilani when something inside me just clicked. Not a dramatic moment. But a quiet knowing that if I waited one more day to feel ready, I'd be waiting forever.

I didn't feel brave when I dialed. I didn't feel strong or inspired or any of the things you see in the movies. I felt scared, tired, and completely unprepared. But I also felt something I hadn't felt in months: Willing.

Willing to admit I didn't know how to fix this alone. Willing to be a beginner again. Willing to let someone else hold my hand while I learned to walk in a different direction.

The woman who answered the phone didn't ask me to explain myself or justify why I deserved help. She didn't require me to prove I was ready or have my life together before they'd work with me. She simply asked a question: "What kind of support are you looking for?"

Not "What's wrong with you?" or "How bad is it?" Just "What do you need?"

That's when I understood something that changed everything. Growth doesn't happen when you're ready. It happens when you're willing.

And willing doesn't require courage. It doesn't require confidence. It doesn't require knowing what comes next or having a perfect plan or feeling excited about the journey.

Willing just requires showing up to the starting line and saying, "I don't know how to do this, but I'm ready to learn."

That phone call led to a 25-week program. Twenty-five weeks of group therapy sessions, individual counseling, and practical tools I didn't even know existed. Twenty-five weeks of sitting in virtual rooms with strangers who understood the weight I was carrying because they were carrying it too.

I approached it like a mission. Not because I was trying to impress anyone, but because my life literally depended on it. Failure wasn't an option. Failure meant death. Or worse, it meant going back to the version of myself I'd left behind.

I completed every homework assignment. Every "i" was dotted, every "t" was crossed. That became my one job: be a good student. Lean in. Participate. Help others. Show empathy, because it doesn't matter what any of us had done—we still mattered. Show love. Learn everything I could. Be a sponge.

But the real breakthrough didn't happen in those sessions. It happened the moment I stopped waiting for permission from my fear and gave it to myself instead.

If you're reading this and waiting for the right time, the right mood, the right amount of courage, or the right circumstances to change your life, let me save you some time: that moment doesn't exist.

The only right time is right now. The only right feeling is willing. The only right condition is exactly where you are.

Your beginning doesn't start when you feel ready. It starts when you finally stop waiting to be ready and decide to begin anyway.

ACTION STEP 1: THE WILLINGNESS ASSESSMENT

Replace "waiting to be ready" with "willing to begin." Identify one area where you can stop waiting and start moving forward this week.

- List 3 areas of your life where you've been waiting to feel "ready"
- For each area, write how long you've been waiting
- Choose the area that matters most to you right now

- Define one small action you can take this week without feeling completely prepared

Your Turn:

The areas where I've been waiting to feel ready:

1. ________________ (waiting for: _____ months/years)
2. ________________ (waiting for: _____ months/years)
3. ________________ (waiting for: _____ months/years)

The area I choose to focus on:

____

One small action I can take this week:

____

When Survival Becomes Your Obsession

The program ended, but I wasn't finished.

When the 25 weeks wrapped up, most people celebrated graduation and moved on with their lives. I couldn't. I sat staring at my computer screen, realizing I still needed my hand held. That thought could have crushed me with shame. Instead, it felt like strength. Maybe asking for more help was its own kind of power.

A month later, I enrolled in a 12-week DBT skills course—Dialectical Behavior Therapy. Not theory. Not pep talks. Practical tools for people who feel everything too much or nothing at all. For people whose emotions run so hot they burn everything down, or so cold they can't feel anything worth living for.

I became obsessed with getting better the same way I had once been obsessed with numbing the pain.

By October 2022, that obsession had spilled into every part of my life. My friend invited me to his wedding, and I had a size 13/14 dress I'd bought for the Air Force Ball the year prior that got canceled due to COVID. I was heartbroken. I never got to wear it, so I made it my goal to drop the weight I had gained over the years from alcoholism just to fit into that dress. I went from 220 pounds to 175 in ten weeks before the wedding. I'd go on to lose another 35 pounds in eight months after that. At my heaviest, I had been 295. The weight loss wasn't about vanity—it was proof.

Proof that I could keep my word to myself. Proof that discipline could rebuild me from the ground up.

When March rolled around, I doubled down. My daughters were one and four, and their father was overseas. It was just us. No help. No safety net. I didn't complain; I didn't whine, because whining wastes energy. I built a strict morning routine—3:30 a.m. wake-up, Mel Robbins's five-second rule to get my feet on the floor before excuses could catch me, then the work—gym, meditation, reading, journaling, and a freezing shower to remind myself I could do hard things before the day even began.

Those years in hermit mode were brutal, but they taught me something no program ever could—how to keep promises to myself. I cut the world off. I set boundaries so sharp they felt extreme. I stopped telling people what I was doing and poured everything into my goals. Those were the years I quit chasing external validation and built my own.

And once again, obsession showed up—not as destruction this time, but as creation.

In November 2022, I started a business with nothing but an idea, a kitchen table, and a bag of Sharpies. I created a stuffed doll in the likeness of my daughters' father, with his image on the front side and his OCP uniform on the back. I posted it on Facebook to one of my craft groups that had, at the time, 1.7 million members. Within three days, it had 6,800 likes. I knew I was onto something. Patent aside, I saw what the doll did for my daughter when we dropped him off at the airport. My three-and-a-half-year-old didn't understand the gravity of the situation until she saw Daddy walking away into the airport, pulling his bags. I will never forget the heartbreak on her face at that moment when she realized he was leaving. He walked through the doors and disappeared.

We cried and hugged it out for a few minutes until we were harshly ushered away to move the truck. As we got in, I gave her "Daddy"—the doll I had finished hand-sewing the night before, because I knew she was going to need it to cope on the drive home. It worked. Immediately, she found solace as she sat in her car seat holding him.

So I went to work. I tore the art off the walls, taped up poster boards, and turned my home into a war room. At 3 a.m., green tea in hand, I'd be standing in front of my scribbles, eyes wild like the Charlie Day meme, asking myself, "What's missing? What do I need to learn next?" I devoured everything—tax structures, bookkeeping, SEO, marketing, branding, customer psychology. It started as a sole proprietorship, but in my mind I was already building the blueprint for millions.

Nothing about those years was balanced. Everything was extreme: the boundaries, the discipline, the pace. I adopted the mindset, "I'm going to die one day," and that urgency lit a fire under me. Every goal became a race against time.

That's what it looks like when survival becomes obsession. It's not graceful. It's not glamorous. It's locking in so hard that people think you've lost your mind, when really you've just decided you're done wasting time. It's moving at an unreasonable pace because you know how quickly life can be stolen. It's pouring every ounce of energy you once spent destroying yourself into building something that finally matters.

And somehow, I never ran out of energy. I don't know if it was the passion for what I was creating, or if I was still running away from death itself. Maybe it was both. Either way, I learned to live at that level and I've never let it go.

Survival rebuilt me. Obsession carried me. And together, they made me unstoppable.

Destruction to Construction

I treated my healing like a lifestyle change, not a quick fix. I knew it was going to take years of work to clean up the mess I'd made for myself.

I got hooked on healing the same way I'd once been hooked on destroying myself.

My obsessive nature hadn't disappeared. It had just found a new target.

Instead of obsessing over when I could drink next, I obsessed over which coping skill to practice. Instead of strategically planning my next blackout, I strategically planned my next breakthrough. Instead of hiding bottles around the house, I hid inspirational quotes and breathing exercises.

Same intensity. Different direction.

That's when I understood something that changed everything: your greatest weakness can become your greatest strength when you point it in the right direction.

My obsession with escape became an obsession with growth. My need to numb pain became a need to feel everything fully and process it completely. My talent for hiding became a talent for deep introspection and honest self-assessment.

I wasn't becoming a different person. I was becoming the person I always had the capacity to be once I stopped using my gifts to destroy myself and started using them to build something worth keeping.

The same military precision that had helped me function while falling apart now helped me rebuild with intention. The same stubbornness that kept me stuck in toxic patterns now kept me committed to healthy ones.

Growth isn't about changing who you are. It's about redirecting who you are toward something that serves your highest good instead of your lowest impulses.

The tools were just tools. The real transformation happened when I stopped fighting my nature and started fighting for it.

ACTION STEP 2: THE INTENSITY REDIRECTION

Channel your most 'toxic' trait toward growth instead of downfall. Turn your greatest weakness into focused healing energy.

- Identify your most intense characteristic (perfectionism, obsessiveness, people-pleasing, etc. Hint: People may have called this your 'toxic' trait in the past)
- Write one way this trait has hurt your relationships or goals
- Brainstorm one way you could use this same intensity for healing
- Commit to redirecting this energy for one week

Your Turn:

My most intense trait is:

____

One way this has hurt me:

____

How I can redirect this toward growth:

____

This week I will use my intensity to:

____

A Toolkit That Saved My Life

We were handed CBT skills, coping tools, and exercises that felt awkward and uncomfortable at first. Some worked, some didn't. But I learned quickly that the only way out was through. I had to test everything until I found what gave me something solid to hold on to.

Mindfulness was one of the hardest things I ever tried, and I hated it at first. Sitting in silence felt unbearable, so I started small. Sweeping the kitchen floor. For two and a half months straight, I swept that floor so mindfully every single day, thinking "this is the stupidest thing ever, what am I even doing?"

Practicing for longer periods each time, focused but not really understanding the point.

Then one random day, I was standing in my kitchen staring out the window, watching the oleanders sway in the wind, and it clicked. Mindfulness. Like a light switch. All at once I knew what it was to be fully present. To actually see beauty without rushing past it.

Breathwork was the same. At first it felt pointless until it started saving me. Regulating my nervous system. Calming the shakes and the panic. It reminded me of what I learned in my military training days: Controlled breathing under pressure, staying focused when everything around you is chaos, and driving forward until you reach your destination.

The difference was, now I was using these skills to save myself instead of simply carrying out someone else's mission.

The Truth About Self-Discovery

Self-discovery is messy. It's sitting with yourself when you'd rather be numb. It's slipping, falling, beating yourself up for not keeping the promise you made to yourself yesterday, then choosing to try again today.

Therapy taught me I'm a good liar—mostly to myself. I held back in individual sessions. I was too ashamed to talk about the things I'd really done. How far I'd let my life spiral, how bad my health had gotten. I sugarcoated the stories. I gave my therapist just enough to show there was pain there, but I kept the ugliest parts locked up.

I was still guarded. It took time. Building rapport, building trust, realizing it was safe to finally get honest. There was no point pretending in that virtual room because the only person I was fooling was myself.

I knew enough back then to recognize that if there was ever a moment to step up, it was right there. The armor I'd been wearing was suffocating me, so I finally laid it down. I did my job. I told the truth. I asked for more help than I was letting on.

That's when the treasure chest cracked open. Gems started spilling out. Insights, breakthroughs, tools I didn't even know existed. I was reintroduced to the power I held inside me. I had no idea then that choosing courage in those moments would make me abundant in ways I couldn't imagine later.

My therapist, Kristi, took me by my virtual hands and led me out of the dark.

The lesson was simple: be honest. Tell them what breaks your heart and why you can't sleep at night. Tell them about the monsters under the bed, the voices in your head, the patterns you can't seem to break no matter how hard you try.

ACTION STEP 3: THE TRUTH TEST

Stop holding back important truths from your support system. Practice radical honesty with one person you trust.

- Identify one truth you've been avoiding sharing with a therapist, coach, or trusted friend

- Choose the person who feels safest to practice honesty with
- Plan when and how you'll share this truth this week
- Remember: the only person you fool by hiding is yourself

Your Turn:

A truth I've been avoiding:

____

The person I trust most to share this with:

____

When I will have this conversation:

____

What I want to say:

____

Goals That Terrify You

Eighteen months into my healing journey, I thought I had growth figured out. I was checking boxes, completing programs, collecting certificates like badges of honor. I felt proud of my progress, my discipline, my ability to stick with the hard stuff.

Then my therapist asked a question that stopped me cold: *"What goal feels so aligned with your soul that it scares you?"*

I sat there for what felt like forever, cycling through my usual answers. Get healthier. Be a better mom. Finish my degree. All good goals. All reasonable. All completely missing the point.

When I finally spoke, the words surprised me—not because they sounded foreign, but because of the conviction behind them: *"To fully trust something bigger than myself."*

I didn't understand exactly what that meant yet. It felt weighty, like stepping into an answer I couldn't fully see. But I knew it mattered. I knew it was deeper than another checkbox. I didn't have the clarity yet, but the gravity of it stayed with me.

Ego Goals vs. Soul Goals

That moment taught me the difference between two kinds of goals that most people never learn to distinguish.

Ego goals always come with conditions. They tell you that you have to prove yourself first. You have to earn it, achieve it, make it look good to the world. They feel urgent and demanding, but underneath they're just afraid of wearing a mask.

Research from Stanford psychologist Carol Dweck shows that people driven by what she calls "performance goals" (focused on looking smart or successful) are more likely to avoid challenges, give up when things get difficult, and experience anxiety about their abilities. They're chasing external validation rather than internal growth.

Soul goals feel completely different. They're quiet. Like whispers you can only hear when you let yourself get still. They don't push you, they pull you. They stretch you past what you think you can handle, not to break you, but to bring you closer to who you're meant to become.

I knew the difference because ego goals drained me while soul goals filled me. Ego goals were about survival. Soul goals were about surrender. One left me empty, the other made me whole.

Faith: The Ultimate Soul Goal

When I finally said it out loud—that my deepest goal was to trust something bigger than myself—I didn't fully understand what I was stepping into. It wasn't about what I could accomplish, but about who I was becoming. It nudged me to loosen my grip on control. To set aside the armor I had worn just to survive. To stop bargaining with my worth.

It pushed me to reimagine what love could look like—not something earned through achievement or perfection, but something steady, something unconditional.

That idea scared me, because surrender asks you to stand without guarantees. To believe you are guided and supported even when you can't prove it or plan it out. To move forward without a backup plan.

Psychology research backs this up. People who approach faith not as a transaction—*if I do this, I'll get that*—but as a way of being in the world report higher levels of resilience, peace, and overall well-being. They see faith as an orientation, not a checklist. But getting there requires a shift: letting go of faith as a tool for outcomes and allowing it to become a transformation in itself.

That's why this became such a soul-level goal for me. It aligned me with something bigger than my own effort or striving. It gave me a kind of peace no title, accolade, or certificate could ever offer. And while I didn't have it all figured out, the pull toward that deeper trust was undeniable.

ACTION STEP 4: THE SOUL GOAL DISCOVERY

Distinguish between goals that drain you (ego goals) and goals that energize you (soul goals) using your body's wisdom.

- List 3 current goals you're pursuing
- Close your eyes and imagine achieving each one
- Notice if your body expands (energized) or contracts (drained) with each goal
- Focus your energy on the goals that make your body expand

Your Turn:

Goal 1: ________________ Body response: Expand/Contract

Goal 2: ________________ Body response: Expand/Contract

Goal 3: ________________ Body response: Expand/Contract

The goal that most expands my body:

____

Why this goal feels aligned with my soul:

____

Growth By Subtraction, Not Addition

This kind of soul-level growth turned everything I thought I knew about goal-setting upside down.

I used to think growth meant proving myself. More achievements, more accolades, more reasons for people to clap and say I was enough. I equated growth with performance. Checking the boxes, always grinding harder for something, climbing ladders that didn't even belong to me.

I thought if I could just do enough, I could finally feel like I was enough. But that version of growth was a trap. It kept me exhausted, empty, and disconnected from myself.

Now I understand that real growth isn't about doing more. It's about alignment. If something doesn't fill my soul or pour back into my cup, I have learned to say no. I've learned that every "yes" you give to something misaligned is a "no" to yourself.

Psychologist Tim Kasser's research on materialism and well-being consistently shows that people who prioritize external goals (wealth, fame, image) over intrinsic goals (personal growth, relationships, community) report lower levels of happiness and higher levels of anxiety and depression. The pursuit of ego goals literally makes us sick.

Soul goals work differently. They don't deplete you because they're connected to your deepest values and authentic self. They energize you even when they challenge you because they're moving you toward who you're meant to be rather than who you think you should be.

The Day I Chose Growth Over Everything I Knew

Two years sober. Tools in my toolbox, healing in my bones, clarity I'd never experienced before. By all outside appearances, I was winning.

But I was still dying inside.

Since January 2019, I had been a stay-at-home mom with Leilani and later, Lillian. I was fully dependent on my ex-husband until I left in November 2023. My world revolved around keeping our home together and raising our daughters, which made me feel even more tied to him. The stability of his paycheck and benefits felt like my lifeline. In many ways, it was.

That dependence made leaving feel impossible. It wasn't just walking away from a marriage. It was stepping out of the only structure I knew to support myself and my girls.

The first time I truly chose growth over comfort was when I left him after 15 years. To anyone looking in, we seemed solid. A long marriage, steady routines, the kind of life people assume means happiness. But inside, I was fading.

The pain of staying finally outweighed the fear of leaving.

When Comfort Becomes Your Prison

I kept telling myself lies that sounded reasonable: "It's secure, be grateful, it could be worse." But comfort without peace isn't comfort at all. And comfort without love is just survival dressed up as safety.

Research shows that people often stay in unsatisfying relationships not because they're happy, but because the fear of change outweighs their dissatisfaction. Psychologists call this "loss aversion"—the tendency to prefer avoiding losses over acquiring equivalent gains. The devil you know feels safer than the angel you don't.

But there's a point where safety becomes suffocation. Where stability becomes stagnation. Where the very thing you think is protecting you starts killing you slowly.

I reached that breaking point on a Tuesday morning in June 2023. My ex called from Europe, once again unloading the same work problems I had already given him solutions for time and time again. Every suggestion I offered fell on deaf ears. He didn't want change—he just wanted to complain. And in that moment, something in me snapped.

By then, I had already outgrown that cycle myself. I'd stopped complaining, stopped whining, stopped nagging. I couldn't stand hearing it anymore. When people came to me with problems, I tried to help them find solutions—not just to fix the issue, but because I couldn't handle the endless noise of staying stuck.

I told him I was done. Done listening, done wasting my energy on someone who didn't respect my time, my grind, my work—any of it. At that point, I was pouring everything I had into my very first business venture, a stuffed doll business I was building from scratch. It mattered to me. It wasn't just a project—it was proof of my commitment to follow through on the goals I had set for myself, to finally build something of my own.

But he never cared to ask about it. The only words he ever offered were dismissive: "Why are you building a business in the middle of a recession?" That one sentence told me everything. My focus, my fire, my alignment—meant nothing to him. I was trying to grow, to build, to expand. And instead of rising with me, he became deadweight, pulling me back while I was fighting to move forward.

When he came home for a month halfway through his short tour in Europe in July 2023, I finally said it out loud. I asked for a divorce. That night, I was asleep in Leilani's twin bed when he came in and sat at the foot of it at 2 a.m. I looked him in the eye and told him I wanted out. No more circling the same fights, no more trying to hold together something that was already gone. We both knew at that moment it was really over. The conversation was short, but it was final.

That was it. The end of a chapter I had been dragging far too long. I was just done. Done pretending that small was enough. Done convincing myself that settling was wisdom. Done living like a guest in my own life. For the first time, I wasn't clinging to what I thought was safe—I was letting go so I could finally step into something real.

Walking away cost me everything familiar. But staying would have cost me everything real.

Military Precision Meets Life Reconstruction

That's when my military training kicked in. I treated the whole thing like a mission. Break it down, assess, rebuild.

In the service, you learn how to operate under pressure. How to adapt fast and how to keep moving even when you're scared. I used those same tactics and instincts on myself. I raised my level of discomfort on purpose, knowing the only way through was forward.

I had to strip my entire world of the old me for it to work. Every piece of my life, tangible or intangible, was put under scrutiny. If it carried heaviness, pain, or old energy, it didn't come with me. Most of it was donated or trashed. There wasn't a scrap of me left behind in that house.

I didn't want the weight of bad memories following me forward, so I thanked it all, let it go with love, and wished it well.

The process was ruthless but necessary. I shed the identity I'd worn for so long: his wife, his partner, his shadow. I let go of the version of me who thought settling was enough. I walked away from friend circles I thought were mine, from personal mementos I swore I could never live without.

When I left, I carried only what felt light, true, and rooted in love.

Stepping out of that life felt like walking into the dark with nothing but a lantern in my hand. Just enough light to see the next step. I couldn't see the whole road, but I didn't need to. Each step was mine, and that was enough.

People don't talk about this part. The terror that comes after you make the right decision. When you're free but floating. When you've burned down your old life but haven't built the new one yet. When you're standing in the space between who you were and who you're becoming.

That space is sacred and terrifying at the same time.

Studies on major life transitions show that people often experience what researchers call "liminality"—the disorienting state of being between what was and what will be. It's uncomfortable by design. Growth requires destruction before reconstruction. You have to demolish the old foundation before you can build on solid ground.

The military taught me something crucial about this phase: you don't need to see the whole mission to complete the next objective. You just need to trust your training, trust your instincts, and keep moving forward.

Identity Purging

In the process, I had to grieve versions of myself I'd been carrying for decades. The people-pleaser who would rather suffer in silence than disappoint someone. The woman who believed her worth was tied to how much she could endure. The person who thought love meant making yourself smaller so others could feel bigger.

I grieved the safety of being invisible. The comfort of letting other people make decisions for me. The illusion that if I just tried harder, gave more, sacrificed deeper, everything would work out.

But grief and relief can exist in the same space. I was mourning the death of who I'd been while celebrating the birth of who I was becoming.

The old me would have stayed. Would have found made up excuses about why leaving was selfish, impractical, or impossible. Would have convinced herself that martyrdom was noble and that her daughters needed to see her endure rather than thrive.

The new me understood that the greatest gift I could give my girls was showing them what it looks like when a woman chooses herself. When she refuses to settle for crumbs because she could have the whole meal. When she trusts herself enough to walk away from what looks good to build what feels right.

Ripple Effects of One Brave Decision

What surprised me most was how one decision created a domino effect in every area of my life. When you stop tolerating what doesn't serve you in one relationship, you stop tolerating it everywhere. When you start honoring your truth in one area, you start honoring it in all areas.

Within months, I wasn't just rebuilding my living situation. I was rebuilding my relationship with myself, my approach to work, my standards for friendship, my vision for the future. Everything shifted because the foundation shifted.

Research on post-traumatic growth shows that people who successfully navigate major life disruptions often report five key areas of positive change: appreciation of life, relating to others, awareness of personal strength, spiritual development, and new possibilities. They don't just bounce back to where they were. They bounce forward to somewhere, and someone, better.

That's exactly what happened. I didn't just survive leaving. I discovered parts of myself that had been dormant for years. Creativity I'd forgotten I had. Dreams I'd buried under practicality. A voice I'd been afraid to use.

The woman who walked away from that marriage wasn't the same woman who had been slowly dying in it. She was stronger, clearer, more connected to her own power. She knew what she wanted and wasn't afraid to go after it.

The Sovereignty You Never Knew You Had

Three years into my healing journey, I finally got quiet enough to truly listen to myself.

When I did, I finally met myself. And what I found wasn't a broken woman, but a strong one. A loving one. A creative one. A woman who had been waiting patiently for me to show up.

In that stillness, in that silence, I found the medicine my soul had been yearning for. The masks I'd worn for so long began to slip, and my true self finally got to breathe. The shame had worn off.

I realized my values weren't about what I'd been told to want. They were about alignment. Alignment with love. With truth. With the woman I was becoming.

The power I own now is sovereignty. For years I gave it away without even realizing it. Handing people the right to tell me who I was, what I was worth, and how far I could go. "You want me to jump? How high?" That was my life's motto back then.

I mistook keeping the peace for love and silence for strength. Every time I abandoned myself like that, I was chipping away at my own soul.

Reclaiming sovereignty didn't look like standing on a hill shouting that I'd arrived. It was quieter than that. It came in the moments I finally said no more. No more shrinking. No more silencing. No more outsourcing decisions that were mine to make.

Sovereignty taught me I don't need permission to live my life. I'm grown. I've got this. Move out of my way.

Sovereignty doesn't make you hard, it makes you whole. It doesn't build walls, it clears them. It makes your love sharper, cleaner, no longer tangled up with resentment or self-abandonment. From this space, nurturing doesn't feel like sacrifice, it feels like overflow.

Now authority doesn't feel like power over anyone. It feels like power within. Steady. Rooted. A quiet confidence that what I bring to my daughters, my loved ones, my clients, is real.

ACTION STEP 5: THE SOUL GOAL DISCOVERY

Take back your decision-making power from others. Make one decision this week without asking for permission or approval.

- Identify one decision you usually ask others to make for you
- Choose to make this decision based on your own judgment
- Notice any urge to seek validation and resist it
- Practice trusting your own authority

Your Turn:

A decision I usually let others make for me:

My decision on this matter:

How it feels to decide without seeking approval:

How "Too Much" Becomes Your Superpower

Pre-sobriety, my intensity was scattered. I'd pour it into the wrong places. Fights that didn't matter, relationships that weren't healthy, proving myself to people who didn't even value me. That's when "too much" felt like a liability. My energy was bleeding out in ways that left me empty.

I learned that intensity itself wasn't the problem. It's how I used it. If I didn't direct it, it was going to continue to run me into the ground.

I saw it clearest in my marriage. I was pouring myself out. Giving everything I had, and in the end I realized I was working toward a retirement I had no say in. Walking toward a future at 50 that I dreaded with everything in me. My nurturing had tipped into neglect, and I lost myself in the process.

When the marriage ended after a brutal 14-month divorce from a man who wasn't even the one I'd married, the pain nearly broke me. Looking back, it was the most beautiful gift I've ever been handed because pain is energy. And energy is just energy. It doesn't matter if you label it good or bad.

At the time I didn't see it, but I was quietly turning every ounce of anger, grief, and heartbreak into momentum. Into power. Into that magma inside me that fuels everything I do today.

The year 2024 is when I realized my superpower. I could transform energy. I felt like a mad scientist who'd just found the formula. I didn't have to wait for "good vibes" or perfect circumstances to manifest something better. I could take the ugliest, darkest energy and flip it to the opposite side of the spectrum. Into joy, love, peace, even bliss through just my thoughts.

Once that clicked, it felt like accessing a whole new level of self-mastery. I could move energy, redirect it, bend it to serve me instead of destroy me. The worst pain became raw material for transformation.

My intensity wasn't the problem. It was the direction. Once I stopped bleeding it out for everyone else and channeled it back into me, it became the very thing that rebuilt me.

The Discipline That Sets You Free

Self-discipline and consistency became two of the biggest muscles I had to build in my healing journey. Discipline is doing the thing even when you don't feel like it. For me it started small. Showing up to every group session, finishing every assignment, not skipping even when my mind and body screamed for the easy way out.

Discipline isn't glamorous. It's gritty. It's saying no to the old patterns and yes to the new ones again and again until it sticks. It's proof to yourself that you can be trusted. That your word to you matters.

Consistency is what makes discipline powerful. Anyone can do something once, but growth comes from stacking wins day after day. For me it looked like showing up to therapy week after week, being mindful even when I didn't want to. The magic wasn't in doing it perfectly. It was in not quitting.

I learned that if you can't keep your own promises, you'll always feel unsteady. The second you start honoring them, no matter how small, you become unshakable. Loyalty to yourself is the foundation for every other part of your life.

Your Beginning Starts Now

You don't have to be ready to begin. You just have to be willing.

Growth doesn't happen when conditions are perfect. It happens when you decide that staying the same is more painful than the uncertainty of change.

Your soul has been waiting patiently for you to get quiet enough to hear what it's been trying to tell you. Your values aren't what you've been told to want. They're what makes you come alive when no one is watching.

Your intensity, your "too much-ness," your obsessive nature—these aren't flaws to fix. They're superpowers waiting for the right direction.

Your past isn't evidence that you're broken. It's proof that you're a survivor. Every pattern you've repeated, every mistake you've made, every rock bottom you've hit—they were preparing you for this moment. The moment you finally choose yourself.

The things you once carried as shame or disqualification can become your fuel. Not just to rebuild your own life, but to help others rebuild theirs. Your mess becomes your message. Your pain becomes your purpose. Your story becomes the bridge someone else needs to cross into their own freedom.

Growth isn't about becoming someone new. It's about becoming who you actually are underneath all the layers of who you thought you had to be.

You already have everything you need inside you. The courage, the strength, the wisdom, the power—it's all there. It's been there all along. You just have to stop waiting for permission to access it.

Your beginning starts now. Not when you feel ready. Not when circumstances align. Not when other people approve.

Now.

YOUR EMERGENCY TOOLKIT FOR GROWTH RESISTANCE

Growth isn't linear, and resistance is normal. When you hit those inevitable moments where you want to quit, others push back against your changes, or doubt creeps in, come back to this toolkit. Fill it out now while you're motivated, so it's ready when you need it most.

When You Want to Quit:

1. Remember your "why"—what drove you to want change? My why:

   ____

2. Take one breath, then one small step My go-to small step when I want to quit:

   ____

3. Ask: "What would the person I'm becoming do right now?" The person I'm becoming would:

   ____

When Others Resist Your Growth:

1. Remember: Their discomfort with your growth is about them, not you. I will remind myself:

   ____

2. Hold your boundaries without explanation My boundary statement:

   "____"

3. Find your tribe—people who celebrate your evolution. People who support my growth:

____

4. Where I can find more support:

____

When You Feel Lost:

1. Get quiet and listen to your soul. My way to get quiet:

____

2. Ask: "What would love do here?" Love would tell me:

____

3. Trust the process even when you can't see the destination. I will trust by:

____

When You Doubt Your Worth:

1. List three things you've already survived:
   a) ____
   b) ____
   c) ____

2. Remember: You don't have to earn your worth—you already have it. I am worthy because:

____

3. Protect your energy like the precious resource it is. I protect my energy by:

____

Notes for when I need extra support:

GROWTH COMMITMENT CONTRACT

I, ______________, commit to owning my beginning by:

- Choosing willing over ready in at least one area this month
- Redirecting my most destructive trait toward growth
- Using my body wisdom to guide my goal-setting
- Taking one major step out of my comfort zone
- Reclaiming my sovereignty in the areas that matter most

My biggest growth edge right now is:

____

The person I'm becoming is:

____

I will know I'm succeeding when:

____

Signature: _________________ **Date:** ___________

Chapter 5: L – Love – Stop Breaking Your Own Heart

For twenty-five years, I lived with someone who hated everything about me.

This voice followed me everywhere. Into job interviews, whispering that I wasn't qualified. Into relationships, pointing out every reason why I didn't deserve love. Into dreams, listing seventeen ways I'd mess it up before I even tried.

Relentless. Cruel. The kind of mean that cuts deep and stays there.

And this voice lived inside my own head.

The cruelest thing fear ever whispered to me was simple: "Don't even try, you'll fail."

For the longest time, I believed it. It felt like all I ever did was fail. At school, at my health, at life. My track record looked like nothing but losses because I was staring at it through a cup of half-empty lenses. I didn't have the perspective to see failure any other way than permanent proof that I wasn't enough.

That voice talked me out of everything that could have changed my life years earlier. It convinced me not to leave toxic relationships sooner because "what if you never find anyone else?" It stopped me from chasing dreams that would have lit me up inside because "you'll just embarrass yourself." It kept me stuck and miserable because "at least this pain is familiar."

I convinced myself it was safer to stay small than to risk looking stupid in front of other people. Fear made failure sound like death. Final, permanent, something I'd never recover from.

But failure isn't death. It's education with tuition paid in bruised pride.

Looking back, I can see exactly what was happening. Every time I gave in to that voice, I was choosing comfort over growth. I was actively participating in the shrinking of myself. How crazy is that? I was my own accomplice in keeping my life small.

The voice wasn't protecting me. It was my prison warden, and I'd handed over the keys.

Men and women alike carry this same cruel narrator. For women, it might whisper about being "too much" or "not enough." For men, it might insist they're "weak" or "failing" at being the provider or protector they think they should be. But the damage is the same—we all become our own worst enemies.

That voice cost me: relationships I was too afraid to fight for, opportunities I was too scared to take, dreams I buried before they had a chance to breathe. Years of my life spent in the waiting room of "someday" because I was too terrified of failing to ever really try.

But the biggest cost wasn't what I missed out on. It was what I did to myself every single day.

I became my own worst enemy. The person who should have been my biggest cheerleader was my harshest critic. The one who should have protected my peace was the one destroying it. The relationship that should have been my safe harbor was the source of my storms.

I was breaking my own heart every single day and calling it self-protection.

The voice had convinced me that being mean to myself would somehow prepare me for when others were mean to me. That if I beat myself up first, it would hurt less when the world did it. That perfectionism was just high standards, and high standards would keep me safe from disappointment.

The truth is, when you're cruel to yourself, you teach everyone else how to treat you. When you don't protect your own peace, you signal that it's not worth protecting. When you break your own heart repeatedly, you normalize heartbreak.

That voice was afraid. Not of me failing, but of me succeeding. Not of me being rejected, but of me being accepted. Not of me looking stupid, but of me discovering how powerful I actually was.

Fear knew that if I ever figured out who I really was underneath all that self-doubt, the game would be over. It would lose its grip. I'd stop listening. I'd start living.

My breakthrough came when I realized the voice wasn't an accurate narrator of my life. It was a scared child who had been put in charge of adult decisions. A trauma response masquerading as wisdom. A protection system that had become more dangerous than anything it was protecting me from.

The day I stopped believing it was the day I started loving myself.

But getting there required something that felt impossible at first: I had to learn to treat myself like someone I actually cared about. I had to stop abandoning myself every time life got difficult. I had to become my own advocate instead of my own prosecutor.

I had to stop breaking my own heart and start healing it instead.

This is the work of the Love phase. Not the Instagram version of self-love that's all bubble baths and positive affirmations. The real work. The daily practice of choosing kindness over cruelty, compassion over criticism, nurturing over neglect.

Learning to love yourself isn't about thinking you're perfect. It's about believing you're worth the effort it takes to grow. It's about treating yourself with the same patience you'd show a friend who's learning something difficult. It's about protecting your peace like the sacred thing it is.

What I wish I knew was that the relationship you have with yourself is the template for every other relationship in your life. How you talk to yourself is how you'll accept being talked to.

How you treat yourself is the standard you'll set for how others treat you. How much you value yourself determines how much value you'll demand from the world.

If you want to change your life, you have to start by changing how you treat yourself. You have to fire the inner critic and hire an inner coach. You have to stop being your own worst enemy and start being your own best friend.

You have to learn to love yourself like your life depends on it.

Because it does.

ACTION STEP 1: THE INNER VOICE AUDIT

Catch your inner critic in action and replace one cruel thought with a compassionate one today.

- Notice when your inner voice gets cruel
- Ask: "Would I say this to someone I care about?"
- Replace the cruel thought with something kinder
- Practice this interruption 3 times today

Your Turn:

The cruel thing I say to myself most often:

____

How I would say this kindly to a friend:

____

My new compassionate replacement phrase:

____

Normalizing Self-Abandonment

The first step to loving yourself is admitting how badly you've been treating yourself.

I don't mean the obvious stuff. Not the drinking or the toxic relationships or the patterns everyone could see from the outside. I mean the quiet, daily ways you abandon yourself that nobody else witnesses.

The way you push through exhaustion instead of resting. The way you eat whatever's convenient instead of what nourishes you. The way you move your body from hatred instead of strength. The way you stay up scrolling when your soul is begging for sleep.

I mean the way you talk to yourself when nobody else is listening.

Treating yourself like someone you actually love starts with the basics. The same way you'd show up for your kids, your best friend, or someone you deeply care about. But first, I had to admit how far I'd fallen from that standard.

For women, this might mean finally resting instead of pushing through exhaustion, or eating what nourishes instead of what numbs. For men, it might mean admitting you need help, or allowing yourself to feel emotions instead of immediately trying to fix or suppress them.

But the pattern is the same regardless of gender: we abandon our own needs to meet everyone else's expectations.

For years, self-abandonment was my default setting. I'd promise myself I'd drink water, then reach for another coffee. I'd swear I'd go to bed early, then pour another glass of wine to keep the night going. I'd plan to eat something nourishing, then grab whatever would numb the feelings fastest.

Every broken promise to myself was a small deception. Every time I chose what was easy over what was good for me, I was teaching myself that my needs didn't matter. That I couldn't be trusted. That I wasn't worth the effort it takes to care for someone properly.

The abandonment went deeper than just physical care. I abandoned my own dreams the second someone questioned them. I abandoned my boundaries the moment they inconvenienced someone else. I abandoned my truth whenever it might have caused conflict.

I was so busy taking care of everyone else that I forgot I was someone worth taking care of, too.

The shift happened when I started asking myself a simple question: "How would I treat someone I love in this situation?"

If my daughter was exhausted, would I tell her to push through? No. I'd encourage her to rest.

If my best friend was hungry, would I tell her to grab junk food? No. I'd suggest something that would actually fuel her body.

If someone I cared about was in pain, would I tell them to numb it with substances? No. I'd help them process it and heal.

But somehow, the rules of love and care didn't apply to me. Self-compassion was selfish. Being hard on myself would make me stronger.

All lies.

Being hard on myself didn't make me stronger. It made me brittle. It made me afraid to try new things because I knew the voice in my head would be ruthless if I failed. It made me settle for less because I didn't believe I deserved more.

The truth is, you can't hate yourself into a life you love. You can't criticize yourself into confidence. You can't shame yourself into change that lasts.

Catching the Little Jabs

The deeper part of stopping self-abandonment was catching the wretched little jabs I threw at myself all day long.

- "You're worthless."
- "You're weak."
- "You'll never get this right."

These weren't dramatic moments of self-hatred. They were quiet, automatic thoughts that ran in the background like malware on a computer. Constantly draining my energy, slowing down my processing, making everything harder than it needed to be.

I had to learn to catch them and replace them with words I'd actually say to someone I loved and nurtured.

"You're trying." "You're learning." "You deserve better."

At first, it felt completely fake. The kind words felt foreign in my mouth like I was speaking a language I didn't know. But repetition is how new programming takes root. Every time I chose compassion over criticism, I was rewiring decades of destructive patterns.

The sickening voice had been so loud for so long that I'd forgotten there were other ways to motivate myself. I thought being mean to myself was necessary. That without the constant criticism, I'd become lazy or complacent.

But the opposite happened. The kinder I became to myself, the more motivated I felt. Not from fear or shame, but from genuine care. When you treat yourself like someone worth fighting for, you start fighting harder. When you treat yourself like someone with potential, you start living up to it.

The voice that had once said, "You'll never amount to anything" started saying, "Let's see what we can do." The voice that had criticized every mistake started celebrating every small win. The voice that had torn me down started building me up.

Not because I was perfect, but because I was trying. And trying to deserve kindness.

From Fake to Fire

I won't lie to you. In the beginning, self-love felt completely fake.

When you've spent decades being your own worst enemy, suddenly becoming your own cheerleader feels like you're performing in a play you don't understand. The words feel wrong in your mouth. The kindness feels undeserved. The compassion feels like lying.

Everything feels fake until it becomes real. Every skill feels awkward until it becomes natural. Every new habit feels forced until it becomes automatic.

I started with the smallest possible acts of self-care. Drinking one extra glass of water. Taking three deep breaths before getting out of bed. Saying "good morning, beautiful" to myself in the mirror even when I didn't believe it.

These tiny rituals felt ridiculous at first. But slowly, something shifted. The tiny habits started adding up. The small acts of love started compounding. The woman I was speaking into existence started showing up in how I carried myself.

What really had to change were my boundaries. For years, I'd said "yes" to everything and everyone, even when it drained me. Learning to say "no" wasn't rejection—it was self-respect. I stopped overextending. I stopped giving away parts of me I couldn't afford to lose.

Slowly, love stopped being something I only gave away and became something I built inside myself. Daily rituals made it real. Mirror work, journaling, movement, even sticky notes around the house reminding me who I was becoming.

It wasn't about perfection. It was about showing up for me every single day the way I'd show up for anyone else I cared about.

The fake became real when I realized that love is a practice, not a feeling. It's what you do, not just what you think. And when you practice loving yourself consistently, eventually your heart catches up with your actions.

That's when the real transformation begins. When self-love stops being something you're trying to do and starts being something you are.

ACTION STEP 2: THE BEST FRIEND CHECK

Treat yourself like your best friend in one area where you've been neglecting your needs.

- Identify one way you've been abandoning yourself this week
- Ask: "How would I care for my best friend in this situation?"
- Take one specific action to care for yourself this way
- Notice how it feels to receive your own care

Your Turn:

One way I've been abandoning myself:

____

How I'd care for my best friend in this situation:

____

The caring action I'll take for myself today:

___

The Mirror Work That Terrified Me

One of the most powerful tools I discovered for learning to love myself was also the one I'd been avoiding for years: looking myself in the eyes.

Mirror work became pivotal in my healing because it forced me to face the one person I'd really been at war with all along—myself. Looking in my own eyes meant taking accountability for my actions. Learning how to smile at my own reflection and mean it.

This practice challenges everyone differently. Women often struggle with physical self-acceptance and perfectionism. Men often struggle with emotional vulnerability and admitting they need encouragement. But everyone struggles with truly seeing themselves as worthy of love and kindness.

In the beginning, it felt unbearable. I couldn't meet my own stare. I couldn't say a kind word and believe it. I was convinced I was the scum of the earth. Unforgivable. Worthless. Every affirmation felt like a lie.

When you do mirror work, there's nobody else in that room but you.

Why was I being so shy? What was I scared of? Who was I hiding from?

I started small. I told myself, "Look in the mirror one time and you never have to do it again if you don't want to." But then I tried again. And again. A little longer each time, shaky voice and all. Talking out loud. It was awkward. Almost painful.

At first, I borrowed affirmations I'd heard from others. Little blueprints for self-talk until I could write my own. I covered my mirrors and walls with sticky notes that read things like "smile." Just the basics. Just a reminder to be nice to myself.

It evolved to things like "you are who you think you are" and reminders that the sky was the limit. Every wall became real estate for reminders that the woman I wanted to be was possible, even if I didn't believe in her yet.

The more I spoke those words, the more I started stepping into them. My actions began to line up with my affirmations. What I told myself in the mirror started showing up in the way I carried myself through the world.

Research from Dr. Kristin Neff at the University of Texas shows that people who practice self-compassion have lower levels of anxiety and depression, greater motivation to improve themselves, and better relationships with others. They also recover quicker from setbacks and are more resilient in the face of failure.

But none of that research mattered to me in those early days. What mattered was that for the first time in my life, I wasn't afraid to look myself in the eye. I wasn't cringing at my own reflection. I was having conversations with myself like I was someone worth talking to.

The breakthrough came when I realized I was actually good company. That the woman staring back at me had been through hell and was still standing. That she was funny, resilient, and worthy of love. Not perfect, but trying. Not flawless, but fighting.

That's when mirror work stopped being about affirmations and started being about recognition. Seeing myself clearly for the first time. Not through the lens of criticism or shame, but through the lens of truth.

ACTION STEP 3: THE MIRROR MOMENT

Look yourself in the eyes for 30 seconds and say one true, kind thing about who you're becoming.

- Find a mirror where you won't be interrupted
- Look directly into your own eyes for 30 seconds
- Say one genuinely kind thing about yourself out loud
- Notice any resistance and do it anyway

Your Turn:

What I saw when I really looked at myself:

The kind thing I said to myself:

How it felt to receive my own kindness:

The Forgiveness Revolution That Set Me Free

The person I needed to forgive most was myself. For the drinking. For staying too long in relationships that broke me down. For abandoning myself over and over again just to keep the peace.

I carried so much shame it was suffocating. No matter how much I tried to point the finger outward, the heaviest weight was always the blame I placed on me.

Forgiveness didn't mean excusing what I'd done. It didn't mean saying, "Oh, it's fine you hurt yourself like that." It meant looking at the version of me who made those choices and realizing she was doing the best she could with what she knew at the time.

Forgiveness was choosing compassion over punishment.

Then came the harder part—forgiving others. My father for the bottle he couldn't put down. My ex-husband for the ways he failed me. People who lied to me or loved me only halfway.

I knew the people I wanted or needed an apology from would never give it to me. No explanation. No justice. No "I'm sorry." At first, I was obsessed. I replayed conversations, ruminated on betrayals, gave my thoughts and my energy away to irrelevance.

I dwelled on the negative because I hadn't yet learned how to shift toward the positive.

Eventually, I stopped waiting. I created my own closure. I took myself out of the game. Instead of chasing balance in people who could never give it, I found it in myself.

That's the difference. Excusing behavior says, "What you did was okay." Forgiving says, "What you did hurt me, but it doesn't get to run my life anymore."

Forgiveness gave me stability. It let me plant my feet again. It gave me back my power. In the end, forgiveness isn't about them. It's about me deciding I deserve to be free.

Research from Dr. Robert Enright at the University of Wisconsin shows that people who practice forgiveness experience reduced anxiety, depression, and anger, while showing improvements in self-esteem, hope, and overall psychological well-being. The physical benefits include lower blood pressure, improved immune function, and better sleep quality.

But forgiveness isn't a one-time event. It's a daily practice. Some days I had to forgive my father all over again. Some days I had to forgive myself for the same mistakes multiple times. Some days forgiveness felt impossible, and I had to settle for "I'm willing to be willing to forgive."

That willingness was enough to start the process. Forgiveness isn't about feeling different immediately. It's about choosing differently repeatedly until the feelings catch up.

ACTION STEP 4: FORGIVENESS

Choose to forgive one person (including yourself) for one specific hurt, not because it was okay, but because you deserve freedom.

- Identify one person you need to forgive (yourself counts)
- Write: "I choose to forgive [name] for [specific action] not because it was okay, but because I deserve to be free"
- Say it out loud three times
- Notice any resistance and choose freedom anyway

Your Turn:

The person I choose to forgive:

____

What I'm forgiving them for:

____

My forgiveness statement:
"I choose to forgive ________________________ for ________________________ not because it was okay, but because I deserve to be free."

When "No" Became a Holy Word

The first time I started saying no out of self-love—and actually meaning it—was at the beginning of 2023. That's when I began enforcing boundaries like never before.

My first purge was on social media. If someone drained me, gave me even a hint of negativity, or just didn't align with where I was headed—delete. No questions. No warnings. No explanations. Just gone.

Month after month, I went on these cleaning frenzies—clearing out person by person, account by account. It didn't stop there, though. I started doing it everywhere in my life: inboxes, contact lists, photos, phone apps, closets, medicine cabinets, filing cabinets. If it felt like clutter, it had to go.

Tangible or intangible—anything that no longer aligned got cleared out. People I once thought I couldn't live without—gone. What was wild was that it got easier every time. Some people circled back asking, "What happened?" But I didn't owe them an explanation. I had already made peace with the truth: every "no" created space for new blessings to walk in, and I wasn't going to waste my energy justifying growth to anyone stuck in my past.

Detachment stopped feeling cold and started feeling necessary. Old energy couldn't walk with me into my new chapter. I had to make room for what was coming.

Deleting, blocking, saying no—it was never about being petty. It was about being free. I was moving out of love. Love for my goals. Love for my family. Love for the woman I was becoming. Boundaries turned into the way I protected that love, and in doing so, I stopped breaking my own heart.

Learning to say no taught me that boundaries aren't walls to keep people out. They're gates to let the right people in. They're not about being mean. They're about being clear. They're not about building barriers. They're about creating sacred space for what matters most.

For years, I'd said "yes" to everything and everyone, even when it drained me. I thought that's what good people did. I thought boundaries were selfish. I thought saying no meant I didn't care.

Every "yes" you give to something misaligned is a "no" to yourself. Every boundary you don't set is a boundary someone else will set for you. Every time you say "yes" when you mean "no," you teach people that your words don't mean anything.

Boundaries became the architecture of my self-respect. They weren't about keeping people out; they were about protecting what I was building inside.

ACTION STEP 5: THE SACRED BOUNDARY SYSTEM

Say "no" to one request or commitment that drains your energy, using a kind but firm boundary script.

- Identify one current drain on your energy
- Choose a boundary script: "That doesn't align with my priorities right now" or "I can't commit to that, but thank you for thinking of me"
- Practice saying no without over-explaining
- Notice how protecting your energy feels

Your Turn:

Something that consistently drains my energy:

____

My boundary script:

"____

____"

How it felt to protect my energy:

____

The Daily Practice of Self-Partnership

Self-love is not a feeling you wait for. Self-love is a partnership you create.

Like any relationship, it requires daily investment, consistent showing up, and choosing each other even when it's not convenient—especially when it's not convenient.

I had to learn to keep my own promises. If I told myself I'd drink water, I drank water. If I said I'd go to bed early, I went to bed early. If I promised myself movement, I moved my body.

Every kept promise built trust with myself. Every broken promise eroded it.

What I discovered is that self-partnership is about reliability. It's about becoming someone you can depend on, someone you'd actually want to be in a relationship with. When you stop ghosting yourself, you stop abandoning yourself. You move from self-doubt into self-trust, from insecurity into stability. It's not about perfection—it's about presence, choosing to meet yourself where you are and proving in small ways each day that you're not going anywhere.

What once felt like my flaws and failures became the very lessons that lit my path—not only to rebuild my own life, but to guide others as they rebuilt theirs. If I could do this, they could do it too. I had everything I needed inside me, and so did they.

When Your Heart Finally Catches Up

For me, self-love didn't arrive with fireworks or some dramatic revelation. It was slower, quieter—more like a deep exhale after holding my breath for years. I can't point to a single day when it switched on, but I can tell you how it felt: less noise in my head, less pressure to perform, less judgment every time I caught my own reflection.

At first, it showed up in the smallest ways. I wasn't nitpicking myself in the mirror the way I used to. I wasn't replaying old mistakes on a loop. I wasn't constantly grading myself against an impossible standard. Instead, I started meeting myself with the same tone I'd use with a friend—neutral, kind, steady.

It wasn't about thinking I was flawless. It was about realizing I didn't need to bully myself into becoming better. The cruel voice still popped up sometimes, but she didn't get to run the show anymore. She became background noise. I could notice her, but I didn't have to obey her.

That shift was everything. It was proof I'd crossed some invisible line—from being my own harshest critic to being someone I could actually rely on. From tearing myself down to standing in my own corner. From questioning if I was worthy to knowing, deep down, that I was.

Self-love stopped being a task I tried to check off a list. It became a relationship I was building with myself. A partnership I could count on.

The relationship with myself had fundamentally changed. I'd gone from being my own worst critic to being my own best advocate. From my harshest judge to my most loyal friend.

This didn't mean I thought I was perfect. It meant I knew I was worthy. Worthy of care. Worthy of kindness. Worthy of fighting for. Worthy of the life I was building.

When you finally learn to love yourself, everything else shifts—the standards you set for how others treat you, the choices you make about where to spend your time and energy, the dreams you allow yourself to chase, the boundaries you maintain to protect your peace.

You stop seeking validation from people who can't see your worth because you're no longer confused about your worth. You stop trying to earn love because you've learned love isn't earned—it's given freely, starting with the love you give yourself.

That's the real transformation of the Love phase. Not learning to think you're amazing, but learning to treat yourself with the basic dignity every human deserves. Not becoming your biggest fan, but becoming your most loyal friend.

The woman who loves herself doesn't need the world to applaud her choices. She doesn't need everyone to understand her journey. She doesn't need external validation to know she's on the right path.

She knows because she's finally listening to the voice that matters most: her own. Not the scared, critical voice that used to run the show, but the wise, loving voice that's been waiting patiently for permission to speak.

When you learn to love yourself, you don't just change your life—you change your legacy. You model for everyone watching that it's possible to choose yourself, to treat yourself well, to build a life from love instead of fear.

And that permission you give yourself? It becomes permission for others to do the same.

That's the ripple effect of self-love. It doesn't just heal you—it heals everyone brave enough to follow your example.

The person reading this right now—whether man or woman—is worth fighting for. Worth the daily practice of love. Worth the effort it takes to unlearn cruelty and learn kindness. Worth becoming their own best friend.

Because when you finally stop breaking your own heart and start healing it instead, you discover something beautiful: you were never broken. You were just waiting for someone to love you back to life. And that someone was always you.

The Love phase is all about treating yourself well in every moment. It's the daily choice to be patient instead of punishing, nurturing instead of neglectful.

Your relationship with yourself is the longest relationship you'll ever have. Make it a good one.

Start with one act of self-love today. Drink water when you're thirsty. Rest when you're tired.

Speak to yourself the way you'd speak to someone you adore.

The person you're becoming is worth every moment of love you give them.

They've been waiting for you to choose them.

Today is the day you finally do.

YOUR SELF-LOVE SURVIVAL PACK

Self-love is a daily practice, not a destination. Your inner critic will test your commitment, and old habits will try to pull you back. Use this survival pack when loving yourself feels impossible. Complete it now so it's ready when your heart needs reminding.

When Your Inner Critic Takes Over:

1. The cruel voice in my head usually says:

   ____

2. The truth I need to hear instead:

   ____

3. Three words that always bring me back to kindness:

   __________________, __________________,

   ____

When Self-Care Feels Impossible:

1. My body is telling me it needs:

   ____

2. The smallest act of care I can give myself right now:

   ____

3. How I'd comfort my best friend in this exact situation:

   ____

When I Question My Worth:

1. Evidence that I am stronger than I think:

   a) I survived: ______________________________

b) I learned: ______________________________

c) I chose growth when: ______________________

2. My worth exists because:

____

When Others Question My Self-Love Journey:

1. What I'll remember about people who resist my growth:

   ____

2. My response when someone criticizes my self-care:

   ____

3. People in my corner who celebrate my healing:

   ____

Chapter 6:
O – Overcome – Breaking the Old Patterns

Your body tells stories your mind refuses to acknowledge.

For decades, I carried pain that doctors couldn't explain and I couldn't understand. My back felt like someone had twisted steel rods down my spine. My legs weighed a thousand pounds on ordinary days. My feet ached like I'd been walking on broken glass, even when I'd barely moved.

The weight clung to me despite every diet, every workout routine, every promise I made to myself. My nervous system lived in a state of constant emergency.

Simple tasks triggered sweating fits that left me embarrassed and confused. Eating lunch with coworkers. Walking to my mailbox. Activities that other people managed without thought turned my body into a furnace of anxiety and exhaustion.

My posture revealed everything I tried to hide. Hunched shoulders, curved spine, head pulled down like a turtle retreating into its shell. I used to joke that I looked like Mr. Burns from *The Simpsons*, all shriveled and bent over. The joke wasn't funny because it was true.

Looking back now, I recognize my subconscious trying to make me disappear. Smaller meant safer. Invisible meant untouchable. If I could shrink enough, maybe the next blow wouldn't find me.

Food became my pharmacy. Emotions got too loud? I'd medicate them with whatever was within reach. It didn't matter if it was healthy or harmful, as long as it muffled the noise screaming inside my head. Each bite pushed the feelings deeper, creating more layers of shame to carry around.

None of this registered as trauma in my awareness back then. This was just my baseline, my normal, the way my body had always operated.

But the reality was more complex and devastating than I wanted to admit. I was housing years of unprocessed survival mode in my flesh and bones. Every unexplained ache, every random sweat attack, every protective slouch was my body communicating what my voice couldn't say.

"Danger lives here. Safety doesn't exist. Someone is always about to hurt me."

Talk therapy gave me vocabulary for the pain, but it couldn't reach what had taken residence in my muscles, my breath, my nervous system's automatic responses. That's where holistic practices became necessary. They addressed something conventional therapy couldn't touch: trauma doesn't just inhabit your thoughts. It moves into your tissue, your breathing patterns, your cellular memory.

When you don't help it find an exit, it stays. Stagnant energy poisoning your system from within.

ACTION STEP 1: BODY AWARENESS SCAN

Notice where trauma lives in your physical body right now.

- Lie down comfortably and close your eyes
- Starting from your head, slowly scan down to your toes
- Notice any areas of tension, numbness, or unusual sensation
- Breathe into those areas without trying to change anything

Your Turn:

Areas where I hold the most tension:

____

What my body might be trying to tell me:

____

One way I can show my body more care today:

____

The Breath That Changed Everything

The practice that brought me home to myself arrived without fanfare or mystical revelation. No retreat center, no guru, no expensive equipment. Just me in my kitchen, finally learning how to breathe like a person instead of a prey animal.

My respiratory system had been stuck in emergency mode so long that shallow, panicked breathing felt completely normal. Chest constricted, shoulders permanently hiked toward my ears, every inhale sharp and brief like I was preparing for impact.

Because I was. I'd been bracing for the next disaster for so many years that hyper-vigilance had become my default operating system.

The first time I deliberately focused on my breathing, the change was immediate and undeniable. Not some mystical transformation, just basic physiology doing what it was designed to do. My shoulders dropped. My jaw released tension I didn't know I was holding. Stop for a moment and check if your jaw is clenched right now. Odds are fifty-fifty that it is, and releasing it will feel like relief you didn't know you needed.

My entire torso softened in ways I'd forgotten was possible.

That's when the truth became crystal clear: I'd been suffocating myself for years. Not just physically, but emotionally and spiritually. Breathwork revealed something profound. Maybe I wasn't fundamentally broken. Maybe I was just exhausted from decades of bracing for impact that never came.

How you breathe reflects how you move through the world. Shallow, rapid breathing signals survival mode. Deep, intentional breathing indicates safety, presence, regulation. When I finally slowed down enough to observe my patterns, I discovered I'd been breathing like someone expecting to be attacked at any moment.

There was always something. Another crisis, another emergency, another reason to stay on high alert. Breathwork became my method of informing my nervous system that the immediate danger had passed. I could release the clench, fill my lungs completely, and actually exhale.

It sounds simple, but relearning how to breathe was relearning how to trust. Trust that I could be present in my body. Trust that this moment was safe. Trust that I didn't have to spend my life preparing for disasters that might never arrive.

Research from respiratory therapists and trauma specialists confirms what I experienced: controlled breathing directly activates the parasympathetic nervous system, shifting you from fight-or-flight into rest-and-digest mode. But for me, the impact went deeper than stress management. Every full breath was a stand against everyone who had ever made me feel like I needed to make myself smaller to survive.

Breathwork reprogrammed my nervous system to stop anticipating catastrophe and start experiencing the present moment. It taught me the difference between being alive and actually living.

ACTION STEP 2: THE BREATH RESET

Practice breathing like you're safe, because you are.

- Sit comfortably and place one hand on your chest, one on your belly
- Breathe so only the bottom hand moves
- Inhale for 4 counts, hold for 4, exhale for 6 counts
- Continue for 2 minutes and notice what shifts in your body

Your Turn:

How I usually breathe:

____

What changed when I breathed consciously:

____

How my body feels when I breathe deeply:

____

How Movement Becomes Medicine

Traditional therapy taught me the "why" behind my pain. Holistic healing taught me the "how" to move it through and out of my system. Some trauma can't be talked through or thought away. It has to be moved through.

Lifting weights until my muscles remembered their strength. Hiking trails until my legs recalled they could carry me anywhere. Running until my lungs burned clean. Dancing barefoot in my kitchen at midnight until my body remembered what joy felt like.

All of it taught me the same fundamental truth: movement is medicine. Your nervous system needs to complete the stress cycles that trauma interrupts.

That's the science behind why you feel genuinely lighter after a good cry or an intense workout. It's not just an emotional release. It's biological. Your system finished the fight-or-flight response that got stuck during the original traumatic event.

For years, I used exercise as punishment. Hated what I saw in the mirror, so I'd torture my body on machines, believing that if I could just inflict enough suffering, maybe I'd finally earn the right to be loved. That approach made everything worse. It was just another way to wage war against myself.

Everything shifted when I started moving from love instead of loathing. Instead of forcing my body through routines designed to punish, I began asking what it actually needed.

Some days it craved lifting heavy things to remember its power. Other days it wanted to dance to reconnect with pure pleasure. Sometimes gentle stretching was all it could handle. Sometimes it just needed to walk outside and feel solid ground beneath its feet.

Movement transformed from warfare into conversation.

Dr. Bessel van der Kolk's groundbreaking research proves that physical practices help people process trauma in ways that talk therapy alone cannot reach. Your body holds the memory of everything that has ever happened to you. Movement gives that memory a voice and, eventually, a way out.

Dancing in my kitchen became a sacred ritual. No audience, no performance pressure, just me and my body remembering what it felt like to move for pure joy instead of survival. Hiking taught me these legs I'd criticized could actually carry me up mountains. Weight training showed me that I could become stronger from resistance, that pressure could build me up instead of break me down.

Movement taught me that healing doesn't always happen when you're stationary. Sometimes you have to shake it off, dance it out, run until you remember who you are underneath all the accumulated fear and pain.

The gym stopped being a place of punishment and became a laboratory for discovering what my body could do when I treated it like an ally instead of an enemy. Every rep became a conversation: "What do you need today?" "How does this feel?" "What wants to move through you?"

My relationship with physical activity completely transformed when I stopped trying to shrink my body and started celebrating what it could accomplish, when I stopped moving from shame and started moving from strength.

ACTION STEP 3: MEASURED MOVEMENT

Ask your body how it wants to move today and honor that request.

- Sit quietly and tune into your physical self
- Ask: "How do you want to move right now?"
- Listen to the first response without judging it
- Move in that way for at least 10 minutes with full attention

Your Turn:

What my body said it wanted:

____

How this movement felt different from exercise:

____

What I learned about my body's wisdom:

____

Breaking Chains That Weren't Mine to Carry

The destructive pattern I chose to interrupt had been passed down through my bloodline long before I took my first breath.

Alcoholism and all its accompanying devastation had woven itself into my family's genetic code across multiple generations. Native blood flows through my veins, carrying the accumulated weight of colonization, systematic displacement, and cultural destruction that obliterated entire communities.

Colonizers stripped away indigenous culture, stole ancestral lands, severed people from their spiritual roots, and then introduced alcohol as a weapon disguised as relief. That poison became a substitute for sacred ceremonies, for authentic connection, for genuine healing practices. By the time it reached me, dysfunction masquerading as normal family behavior was all I knew.

Bottles hidden in unlikely places throughout the house. Laughter used as a mask for profound hurt. Everyone participating in the collective pretense that the slow-motion suicide happening in plain sight was just how families functioned.

Initially, I assumed the problem was personal failure. I was weak, I was defective, I couldn't handle what everyone else seemed to manage effortlessly. It required getting genuinely quiet and looking beyond surface explanations to recognize this wasn't entirely mine to own. This was inherited trauma, transmitted across generations of people who were never given access to healthy coping mechanisms.

I was carrying their unprocessed shame, their learned self-destruction, their enforced silence. But those burdens didn't belong to me. What belonged to me was the power to choose differently. To interrupt the cycle. To plant my feet firmly and declare, "This pattern ends with me."

My father died at forty-five from complications directly connected to alcohol abuse. Forty-five years old. That reality struck me like lightning when I turned thirty-six and recognized

I was walking the identical path. I refused to pass that same legacy to my daughters.

The day I stopped drinking marked more than just putting down the bottle. It represented teaching myself completely different ways to process emotional pain. Breathwork instead of numbing. Physical movement instead of paralysis. Actually feeling instead of running away from difficult emotions.

That's when I understood that personal healing is fundamentally radical. By choosing to confront myself instead of escaping into substances, I was authoring an entirely different story for my daughters to inherit. One grounded in emotional strength and authentic truth instead of generational wounds and imposed silence.

Research on epigenetics demonstrates that trauma can literally be transmitted through family lines at the cellular level. Healing can be transmitted too. When you successfully break a destructive pattern, you don't just transform your own life. You alter the trajectory of everyone who comes after you.

My daughters will never have to wonder if it's possible to choose sobriety over addiction, healing over numbing, courage over avoidance. They'll have watched their mother do it. They'll carry that possibility in their bones instead of carrying the weight of inherited trauma.

What you don't question, you repeat. What you consciously interrupt, you transform. The patterns you break today become the freedom your children inherit tomorrow.

ACTION STEP 4: GENERATIONAL CURSE BREAKING

Identify one inherited pattern you're ready to interrupt and take concrete action to break it.

- Name one destructive pattern you inherited from your family
- Identify specific ways this pattern has shown up in your own life
- Choose one different action you can take this week to break the cycle
- Remember that healing this pattern serves everyone who comes after you

Your Turn:

The inherited pattern I'm ready to break:

____

How this pattern has affected my life:

____

One specific action I'll take to break this cycle:

____

The legacy I want to create instead:

____

Integrating Logic and Intuition

Most of my adult life was spent existing in rigid black-and-white thinking. If something couldn't be measured, controlled, or logically proven, I wanted nothing to do with it. My military background reinforced this approach to life. Everything had to be concrete, structured, demonstrable.

Spirituality, it felt dangerous because it lived in gray areas that made me profoundly uncomfortable. My family had experiences with metaphysical phenomena I didn't want to understand or acknowledge, and that terrified me. Even during my weather forecasting training, uncertainty triggered anxiety attacks. Being asked to predict atmospheric conditions that weren't guaranteed felt impossible and wrong.

That same discomfort extended to faith and spiritual practices. Too vague, too intangible, too impossible for my logical mind to categorize and control.

But when I started incorporating meditation and mindfulness into my daily routine, slowing down enough to actually inhabit my body instead of constantly trying to escape it, something fundamental shifted. I began accessing aspects of myself that had been buried under decades of striving and controlling.

What I discovered was feminine energy in its most authentic form: creativity, softness, nurturing instincts, natural flow, intuitive wisdom, healing capacity. The more space I created for stillness instead of constant motion, for creativity instead of pure achievement, for softness instead of force, the more connected I felt to something larger than my individual struggles and ambitions.

Call it God, universal energy, higher consciousness, ancestral wisdom. The specific terminology matters less than the experience itself. For the first time in my life, uncertainty didn't fill me with panic. It felt like coming home to myself.

What ultimately saved me was learning the art of surrender. The approach I'd always assumed would make me weak actually became the source of my genuine strength. Releasing the illusion of control, admitting I didn't possess all the answers, trusting what I couldn't see or scientifically prove.

What definitely didn't work was attempting to force my way through healing like it was another military mission to complete efficiently. Everyone says "just push through the pain," but that strategy left me more depleted and disconnected than before I started.

True healing required the opposite approach entirely. Slowing down, becoming softer, breathing consciously, allowing myself to actually feel emotions instead of immediately trying to solve or escape them. I learned that you can't think your way into wholeness. You have to feel your way there, love your way there, surrender your way there.

If you've been operating primarily from the logical, analytical, problem-solving side of your mind, you're running on partial power. Authentic healing invites you to integrate both aspects of human intelligence: structure and flow, logic and intuition, discipline and creativity, masculine and feminine energies.

When you achieve that balance, that's when you discover genuine alignment. Your head and heart working together instead of constantly fighting each other for dominance.

The military taught me how to function under extreme pressure, how to complete missions even when I was scared or uncertain. Those skills served me well during the structured aspects of recovery. But healing also required me to access parts of myself that the military had never addressed: intuitive wisdom, emotional intelligence, spiritual connection, creative expression.

Learning to integrate both sides of my nature didn't mean abandoning the strengths I'd developed. It meant adding new dimensions to who I was becoming. Logic and intuition working as partners instead of competitors.

ACTION STEP 5: INTEGRATION

Practice accessing whichever side of yourself (logical or intuitive) you typically avoid.

- If you usually rely on logic: spend 10 minutes in nature without trying to solve anything
- If you usually follow intuition: create a concrete plan for one area of your life
- Notice which approach feels uncomfortable or unfamiliar
- Use both approaches to make one decision this week

Your Turn:

I typically rely on (logic or intuition):

When I tried the opposite approach, it felt:

How I can use both in decision-making:

One decision where I'll practice integration:

The Alchemy of Energy Transformation

Pain doesn't vanish just because you pretend it isn't there. It lingers in the body, changes form, and waits for direction. Anger, grief, heartbreak, fear—they're all energy. And energy, by its nature, can be transformed. The same current that burns can also illuminate, depending on how you choose to channel it.

That's what I came to understand: the emotions that felt like they were sabotaging me could be redirected into something that served me. What once felt destructive could become creative power.

Daily rituals became containers for that energy, giving it shape and direction. Painting offered my feelings a place to land. Meditation created space between me and my thoughts.

Walking barefoot reminded me I belonged to something larger than my individual pain. These weren't escapes—they were reminders that I wasn't powerless.

The transformation began when I stopped treating pain like an intruder and started treating it like raw material. Tears watered resilience I didn't know I was growing. Anger became fuel for boundaries that actually protected me. Heartbreak revealed what real love would need to look and feel like.

That's the essence of alchemy: not erasing the hurt, but transmuting it into purpose. The anger of being abandoned sharpened my advocacy for those still abandoning themselves. The shame of addiction softened into compassion for anyone still in the fight. The fear of not being enough hardened into a commitment to remind others of their worth.

Every fragment of pain became part of my strength. Every wound opened the door to wisdom. Every breakdown laid the groundwork for a breakthrough.

This is the secret of energy work that most people never discover: emotions aren't garbage you throw away. They're compost. Left unattended, they rot. But if you work with them, they break down into something that nourishes new growth.

The pain that once threatened to undo me became the very thing that equipped me to help others heal. My mess became my message. My wounds became the credentials that let me sit eye to eye with someone else's suffering and say, *"I get it. And you can get through it."*

The process wasn't neat or linear. Some days I still wanted to check out instead of transform. Some feelings felt too heavy to touch. But over time, I learned a truth that changed me—every emotion carries intelligence, every hard experience carries medicine, and every wound holds the possibility of becoming wisdom.

By 2024, I finally understood this as a skill, not a fluke. I didn't need perfect conditions or a "good mood" to create change. Whatever energy surfaced, I could catch it, shape it, and put it to work for my growth.

That realization was liberation. Pain became the teacher. Darkness became fertile soil. And the very emotions that once threatened to undo me became the ground where transformation could finally take root.

Rewriting the Future Without Erasing the Past

I used to fantasize about getting a completely clean slate. Erasing the traumatic memories, cutting out the painful experiences, starting over with no scars or emotional baggage to weigh me down.

But healing doesn't operate that way. You don't get issued a brand-new life with no history attached. You get the same life that's been marked and shaped by everything you've experienced. The work involves writing a new story on top of the existing one, not erasing what came before, but consciously choosing what deserves to remain in focus.

This means I carry my entire history with me every single day, but not as dead weight dragging me backward, but as accumulated wisdom that informs my choices and strengthens my foundation. When fear shows up, I don't automatically push it away anymore. I ask what it's here to teach me, what it wants me to notice or prepare for.

When shame attempts to hijack my thoughts, I remind it that the woman who made those old choices isn't running the show anymore. She did the best she could with the resources and knowledge she had at the time. Her struggles taught me how to make better decisions. Her pain became the foundation for my compassion.

When my daughters observe me setting boundaries, speaking difficult truths, or walking away from situations that don't align with my values, they're witnessing their family's future being rewritten in real time. They're learning that it's possible to honor the past without being imprisoned by it.

Healing looks like using the same mind that once spiraled in chaos to create clear visions and concrete strategies that actually serve my highest good. It looks like recognizing old patterns before they take control and consciously choosing different responses, even when those responses feel awkward or uncertain.

It's not about pretending painful events never happened. It's about using them as the foundation for building the life I actually want to live.

Healing isn't erasure. It's sophisticated alchemy. You don't throw your history away like trash. You transform it into wisdom, determination, proof that you can survive absolutely anything and still choose to thrive.

Every single day I get to decide how to interpret and use my experiences. That ongoing choice is what rewrites the future without dishonoring the past.

The patterns you successfully interrupt today determine what emotional inheritance you leave your children. The cycles you courageously break right now decide where generational trauma stops flowing forward. The healing work you commit to in this moment creates the legacy that will outlive your physical presence in this world.

My past gave me depth, resilience, empathy, and qualification to help others navigate similar struggles. I wouldn't erase it even if I could, because it shaped me into someone capable of transforming pain into purpose, wounds into wisdom, trauma into triumph.

The Moment Your Body Finally Trusts You

The moment I knew I had truly overcome wasn't marked by the absence of pain. Pain doesn't disappear completely. It transforms into something useful. The moment I recognized my transformation was when I stopped being controlled and limited by pain and started being empowered and motivated by it.

When I stopped asking, "Why did these terrible things happen to me?" and started asking, "How can I use these experiences to help other people heal?"

When I stopped hiding my scars like shameful secrets and started sharing my story as evidence that recovery is possible.

When I stopped viewing trauma as my permanent limitation and started seeing it as my qualification to guide others through their own healing processes.

That's when overcoming stopped being something I was desperately trying to achieve and started being something I naturally embodied. When breaking destructive patterns became my core identity instead of just another item on my self-improvement to-do list.

The woman who has learned to overcome doesn't pretend she never fell down. She uses her experience of falling as proof that she knows exactly how to get back up. She doesn't hide her wounds like something to be ashamed of. She shows others how wounds can be transformed into wisdom.

She doesn't minimize her pain or pretend it didn't matter. She maximizes the purpose that pain can serve.

That's the crucial difference between merely surviving difficult experiences and truly overcoming them. Surviving means you got through it and you're still breathing. Overcoming means you got through it, learned from it, grew because of it, and now you're helping others do the same.

Your nervous system knows how to regulate itself when you give it the right conditions. Your body knows how to heal when you stop fighting against it and start working with it. Your spirit knows how to rise when you stop trying to force the process and start trusting the timing.

The patterns that have held you captive are losing their grip on your daily reality. The cycles that have controlled your choices are being interrupted by your conscious decisions. The invisible chains that have bound you to old ways of being are breaking apart, link by link.

The woman you're becoming through this healing process isn't just someone who has overcome trauma. She's someone who helps others overcome theirs. Not just someone who broke free from destructive patterns. She's someone who shows others how to break free from theirs.

CHAPTER CHECKPOINT: THE PATTERN BREAKER ACTIVATION

Part 1: Body Awareness Assessment (10 minutes)

- Do a full body scan from head to toes
- Notice where you hold tension, pain, or numbness
- Write down what your body has been trying to tell you
- Commit to one daily practice that helps your body feel safe

Part 2: Breathing Reset Protocol (15 minutes)

- Practice the 4-count inhale, 6-count exhale technique for 10 breaths
- Notice how your nervous system responds to conscious breathing
- Set 3 daily phone alarms to check and reset your breathing
- Track how intentional breathing affects your stress levels

Part 3: Movement Medicine Plan (20 minutes)

- List 5 ways you could move your body that feel good, not punishing
- Try each one for 2 minutes and notice what happens emotionally
- Choose the movement that helps you feel most connected to yourself
- Schedule this movement medicine into your week like a prescription

Part 4: Generational Pattern Breaking (15 minutes)

- Identify one toxic pattern from your family that you're ready to break
- Write exactly how this pattern has affected your life
- Choose one specific action you can take this week to interrupt this cycle
- Write a letter to future generations about the pattern you're breaking

Part 5: Energy Alchemy Practice (10 minutes)

- Think of one painful experience that still affects you
- Write 3 ways this experience made you stronger or wiser
- Identify how you could use this wisdom to help someone else
- Take one action this week to transform your pain into someone else's hope

YOUR REBEL HEALING TOOLKIT

Healing is an act of rebellion against everyone who taught you to stay small, stay silent, stay stuck. When the old patterns try to reclaim you, use this toolkit to remember your power.

When Your Body Feels Unsafe:

1. My body is trying to tell me:

   ____

2. I can help my body feel safe by:

   ____

3. The breath pattern that calms my nervous system:

   ____

When Old Patterns Try to Return:

1. The pattern that's trying to resurface is:

   ____

2. This pattern served me when:

   ____

3. But it no longer serves me because:

   ____

4. Instead of this old pattern, I choose:

   ____

When I Feel Overwhelmed by Emotions:

1. These intense feelings are energy that wants to create:

   ____

2. I can move this energy through my body by:

____

3. This energy is trying to teach me:

____

When I Question My Healing:

1. Evidence that I'm breaking generational patterns:

   a) I now ______________________________________

   b) I no longer _________________________________

   c) I'm teaching others ___________________________

2. The person I'm becoming is:

____

3. My healing serves something bigger than myself by:

____

Chapter 7:
W – Wisdom – Becoming Her

She glides through the produce section like it's her personal runway—headphones in, hips swaying to music only she can hear. The woman I was always meant to be doesn't ask permission to take up space or apologize for finding joy in the most ordinary places.

She laughs at her own jokes because laughter doesn't need an audience to be valid. She speaks for those whose voices tremble too hard to advocate for themselves. She maintains high standards not out of perfectionism, but because she embodies the integrity she expects from the world.

This woman pulls her weight completely, shows up with her whole heart, and expects the same commitment from the people around her—not from ego or entitlement, but from deep respect for the energy she pours into every interaction.

She is sensual without apology, grounded in her power, authentic to her core. She no longer chases validation because she knows now—validation isn't oxygen. She breathes from a well within herself that never runs dry.

Even in my hardest seasons, I always sensed something powerful living inside me. A flame that flickered in the dark. A force that whispered there was more—more to contribute, more to create, more to become. That flame never went out, even when chaos and fear tried to smother it. For decades, I kept it small, terrified of what might happen if I let it burn without restraint. But that fire was never designed to stay contained. Now she lets it blaze at full capacity.

Part of unlocking this power was embracing what I call my dark feminine energy. Not in some mystical or esoteric sense, but in the very practical, tangible way of learning to inhabit my own skin with confidence and pleasure.

I had spent years being self-conscious about all the wrong things—hiding my body, questioning my beauty, avoiding mirrors like they might reveal something shameful. Healing showed me that confidence isn't arrogance—it's ownership. Owning my presence in any room. Owning my beauty without waiting for permission. Understanding that pleasure and power belong in the same woman.

Once I allowed myself to enjoy being in my own skin, new doors opened. People responded differently. Rooms shifted. Energy rearranged itself around the certainty I carried.

I stopped pretending I didn't understand my power. I stopped shrinking so others could feel comfortable with my intensity.

She—the woman I've become—is fierce in her convictions, steady in her values. A storyteller who turns scars into lessons. An educator who spins pain into wisdom. A leader who doesn't just rise but makes space for others to rise alongside her.

She's magnetic, not because she seeks attention, but because authenticity speaks louder than performance ever could.

The old version of me believed this woman was "too much." Too passionate about what mattered. Too loud about what was unjust. Too opinionated about my own life. But shrinking never protected me. Making myself smaller never kept me safe. It only robbed me of who I was born to be.

So I chose differently. I flipped the script entirely. My passion became my signature flavor. My intensity became the unique quality nobody else could replicate. My fire became the beacon others could follow when they needed to find their own light in dark times.

This is her: the woman who wields everything—her wisdom, her scars, her joy, her convictions—as both shield and invitation.

She doesn't chase relationships, opportunities, or recognition. She attracts what resonates with her essence. Her energy speaks before she does. Her presence shifts the atmosphere.

I don't beg for respect. I radiate it so consistently that it can't be ignored. Real power doesn't come from forcing outcomes or proving worth—it comes from inhabiting who you already are.

This is the woman I was always meant to be. Not waiting to be noticed. Not asking to be validated. But standing so fully in her essence that overlooking her is impossible.

ACTION STEP 1: STEP INTO YOUR AUTHENTIC SELF

Identify the qualities you've been hiding because you were told they were "too much."

- List 3 aspects of your personality others have called "too intense"
- Reframe each one as a strength rather than a flaw
- Choose one quality to express more fully this week
- Notice how authenticity affects your energy and interactions

Your Turn:

Qualities I've been told are "too much":

1. ______________________________
2. ______________________________
3. ______________________________

How I can reframe these as strengths:

1. ______________________________
2. ______________________________
3. ______________________________

The quality I'll express more fully this week:

____

From Mess to Message: The Alchemy of Purpose

I used to treat my pain like baggage I had to drag behind me everywhere I went—something to hide, minimize, or bury under whatever smile I could manage to paste on my face.

Pain doesn't disappear just because you ignore it. It lingers in your body, influences your choices, colors your voice—until you finally decide to face it directly and transform it into something useful.

The shift occurred when I stopped locking painful experiences away and started speaking pieces of my story out loud. At first, the sharing felt small and tentative—a comment during group therapy, opening up to a trusted friend, journaling thoughts I'd never spoken aloud.

Something unexpected began happening. People would nod with recognition, tear up with shared understanding, or whisper *"me too"* in response to my vulnerability.

That's when the realization hit me: my mess wasn't uniquely mine.

The shame I carried about my relationship with alcohol? Half the people in that therapy room were fighting the same battle with substances or other addictive behaviors. The fear I harbored about not being fundamentally worthy of love? That soundtrack was playing in their heads too. The trauma patterns I thought made me irreparably broken? They were struggling with similar cycles of self-destruction and healing.

My personal pain had found its community. And if my pain had company, maybe my healing process could serve a greater purpose than just my individual recovery.

That's when I began seeing my most shameful experiences differently. The things I wanted to hide became the very things that could help others heal. The experiences I once viewed as disqualifications became my qualifications for understanding what other people were going through.

I stopped interpreting pain as failure and began reading it as testimony. Each hardship became a lesson worth passing on, each breakthrough a signpost I could point to for others finding their way.

This transformation didn't happen overnight. It took time to trust that sharing my story could actually serve others rather than just expose my vulnerabilities to judgment or rejection.

But gradually, consistently, I learned to alchemize every difficult experience into wisdom that could light the way for someone else. The regret I carried became clarity about the choices I make now. The doubt that used to paralyze me became faith in my ability to figure things out. The envy I once felt watching others thrive became inspiration to create my own version of success.

What I once thought would break me became the raw substance of the woman I was becoming. Pain turned into purpose. Scars turned into strategies. And the very moments I wanted to erase became the reasons others could trust me to guide them through their own fire.

Research on post-traumatic growth shows that people who find meaning in their experiences by helping others often demonstrate significantly better long-term recovery. When we transform personal pain into service, we don't just heal ourselves more completely—we accelerate the process through the act of contribution.

My mess became my message not through a dramatic revelation, but through the consistent choice to use every difficult experience as fuel for understanding, empathy, and practical support for others walking similar paths.

ACTION STEP 2: EXTRACTING YOUR PURPOSE

Identify how your most difficult experiences have qualified you to help others.

- Write about one painful experience you've overcome or are overcoming
- List 3 ways this experience has made you stronger or wiser
- Identify how you could use this wisdom to support someone else
- Take one action this week to transform your pain into someone's hope

Your Turn:

A difficult experience I've navigated:

____

Three ways this made me stronger or wiser:

- ______________________________________
- ______________________________________
- ______________________________________

How I could use this wisdom to help others:

____

One action I'll take this week to serve others:

____

Designing a Life You Actually Want to Live

For most of my adult life, I was an expert at designing escape routes instead of designing a life worth staying in.

I constantly strategized ways to get out of my current relationship, endure my present job, or survive whatever phase I found myself trapped within. My existence felt like a series of temporary situations I was white-knuckling through until something better materialized.

But "something better" never arrived organically because I wasn't consciously creating conditions for it to emerge. I was surviving what stood in front of me rather than building what I actually wanted.

The fundamental shift happened when I stopped asking "How do I escape this situation?" and started asking "How do I create what would actually fulfill me?"

When I stopped designing exits and started designing entrances. When I stopped planning escapes and started planning expansion.

This represents the essence of the wisdom phase. Not just healing from past wounds, but consciously constructing future possibilities. Not just breaking destructive patterns, but building life-giving ones. Not just surviving your history, but architecting your destiny.

Most people think life design involves vision boards and goal-setting workshops. Those tools can be helpful, but they're not the foundation. The foundation is knowing who you are underneath all the programming you've absorbed from family, society, and personal survival mechanisms.

When I finally got quiet enough to listen to my own voice instead of everyone else's opinions about what my life should look like, I discovered I'd been living someone else's definition of success. Someone else's idea of what would make me happy. Someone else's dreams dressed up as my own aspirations.

No wonder I felt constantly restless and dissatisfied. I was trying to inhabit someone else's vision for my life.

The real design work began when I gave myself permission to want what I actually wanted. To value what genuinely mattered to me. To dream dreams that felt authentic to my core instead of impressive to other people.

I wanted to laugh genuinely every single day. I wanted to feel useful and contribute to something meaningful. I wanted to make a positive difference in people's lives. I wanted my daughters to witness a woman who loved her life instead of someone who was merely surviving it.

Simple desires, but revolutionary for someone who had spent decades living for external approval and validation.

Research from Stanford's Life Design Lab demonstrates that people who approach their lives like designers—prototyping, experimenting, iterating based on results—report significantly higher life satisfaction than those who try to plan their way to happiness through rigid goal-setting alone.

Life design isn't about creating a perfect plan and executing it flawlessly. It's about developing a clear vision and being willing to experiment your way toward it through conscious choices and course corrections.

For me, this meant trying activities I'd never considered before. Initiating conversations that felt risky but important. Taking calculated risks that aligned with my values even when the outcomes weren't guaranteed.

It meant designing daily routines that energized rather than depleting me. Cultivating relationships that supported my growth rather than sabotaging it. Choosing work that fulfilled my sense of purpose rather than just meeting my financial obligations.

Most importantly, it meant creating a life so aligned with my authentic self that escape wasn't even a consideration anymore. When you're living in alignment with your core values and designing experiences that nourish your soul, you don't fantasize about running away. You wake up excited to engage with what you've built.

The choice between comfort and growth becomes obvious when you realize that growth is the path to sustainable fulfillment, while comfort without purpose leads to stagnation and regret.

ACTION STEP 3: YOUR LIFE DESIGN PROTOTYPE

Create a small experiment to test one aspect of your ideal life vision.

- Identify one element of your dream life you could test on a small scale
- Design a one-week experiment to try this element
- Notice what energizes you and what feels forced or misaligned
- Use the results to inform you of your next life design choice

Your Turn:

One element of my ideal life I want to test:

____

My one-week experiment will involve:

___

What I expect to learn from this experiment:

___

How I'll use the results to inform my next choices:

___

Owning Your Power Without Apology

What I came to understand was that power isn't measured by how much you can endure—it's measured by how wisely you invest it. For years, I treated my energy like an unlimited resource, handing it out without intention. But energy is currency. Where you spend it determines the return you get back.

Real mastery came when I stopped asking, *"How much can I take on?"* and started asking, *"Does this deserve me?"* That single shift changed everything.

I learned that true power requires rhythm. Push and pull. Expansion and rest. The same way a muscle needs recovery to grow, your inner fire needs recovery to stay lit. Burnout taught me that intensity without rest is just erosion. Sustainability, not survival, became my new measure of strength.

2024 was the year I started practicing alignment over effort. Instead of grinding myself down to prove I was strong, I began listening to my body, my intuition, my nervous system. If my chest tightened every time I walked into a situation, I paid attention. If something brought a sense of calm expansion, I leaned in. That awareness became my compass.

I realized power isn't about being unshakable all the time. It's about knowing how to recalibrate when life shakes you. It's being able to self-correct—to bring yourself back into balance instead of waiting for someone else to rescue you.

That's what sovereignty really looks like—not control, not domination, but self-responsibility. Knowing your worth so deeply that you stop trading your energy for scraps. Honoring yourself enough to say no when something isn't aligned, and trusting that what is aligned will meet you when you hold your ground.

Instead of apologizing for my passion, I started treating it like the asset it had always been. My fire became my edge, my proof that I was fully alive and deeply committed to what mattered. The moment I stopped apologizing for who I was, I stopped attracting people who wanted a watered-down version of me.

My circle got smaller, but it became exponentially more authentic. I started walking into rooms focused on being completely myself rather than worrying about being perceived as "too much." That supposed character flaw became the exact quality that made me magnetic to aligned people and opportunities.

The aspects of yourself you're most afraid to reveal are usually the ones holding your greatest power. Don't apologize for your light just because someone else hasn't yet developed the capacity to stand in its brightness.

ACTION STEP 4: TAKE THE WHEEL BACK

Identify where you've been giving away your power and reclaim it consciously.

- List 3 situations where you shrink yourself to make others comfortable
- Identify one area where you apologize for being "too much"
- Practice expressing this quality with confidence this week
- Notice how owning your power affects your relationships and opportunities

Your Turn:

Situations where I shrink myself:

1. ______________________________
2. ______________________________
3. ______________________________

An area where I apologize for being "too much":

____

How I'll practice owning this power this week:

____

What I expect to change when I stop apologizing:

____

Your Success Evolution

My definition of success has undergone a complete transformation through this healing journey.

There was a time when I chased achievement for the sake of achievement. I worked harder, checked more boxes, and reached for goals that looked impressive but didn't actually fulfill me. On the outside, it seemed like progress. On the inside, it felt empty.

Healing shifted that perspective. Success stopped being about pushing harder and started being about alignment. It became less about how much I could accomplish and more about whether my choices reflected my values. If an opportunity drained me or pulled me out of integrity, I learned to let it go—no matter how impressive it might have appeared to others.

Now success means choosing what sustains me and allows me to contribute in ways that feel true. It's not about being the most accomplished. It's about being the most authentic.

The old version of success asked: *"How can I impress them?"* The evolved version asks: *"How can I honor myself?"* The old version measured achievement by external metrics and comparison. The new version measures fulfillment by inner peace and genuine contribution.

The old version demanded constant proving and performing. The new version requires deliberate choosing—alignment over approval, authenticity over image, truth over comfort.

This is the kind of success that transforms life from the inside out. Not the kind that makes you look impressive to strangers, but the kind that leaves you genuinely satisfied with who you are becoming and how you choose to show up in the world.

ACTION STEP 5: REFRAME "SUCCESS"

Define what success means to you now, separate from external expectations.

- Write your old definition of success (what you used to think mattered)
- Write your new definition of success (what actually brings fulfillment)
- Identify one area where you're still chasing old success metrics
- Make one choice this week that aligns with your new definition

Your Turn:

My old definition of success was:

____

My new definition of success is:

____

An area where I'm still chasing old metrics:

____

One choice I'll make this week that aligns with my authentic success definition:

The Discipline of Becoming

Discipline isn't about harshness or rigidity—it's about structure that frees you. Consistency isn't about perfection—it's about building enough repetition that your actions carry you even when motivation fades. Together, they create reliability, the foundation every transformation rests on.

Self-discipline taught me that growth doesn't happen in big, dramatic moments but in the small, ordinary choices you repeat until they shape your life. Consistency is how those choices take root. It's what turns vision into reality, one steady step at a time.

Through this lens, I began to see discipline not as punishment, but as devotion. Devotion to my future self. Devotion to the values I wanted to embody. Each time I stayed the course—especially when quitting would have been easier—I was proving to myself that I could be trusted to carry my own potential forward.

Stability came when my actions lined up with my intentions. Following through, even on the smallest commitments, created an inner steadiness that nothing external could shake. What once felt like self-denial became self-respect. Self-loyalty wasn't selfish—it became the foundation for every other healthy relationship and responsibility in my life.

Research from Dr. Angela Duckworth on grit and perseverance shows that consistency of effort over time predicts meaningful achievement more accurately than talent or intelligence. The people who create lasting change aren't always the most gifted—they're the ones who keep showing up, especially on the days when it feels hardest.

But discipline isn't about becoming robotic or ignoring your own needs. It's about becoming dependable to yourself. It's about aligning actions with values, even when moods shift or circumstances change.

Every time you choose aligned action over comfortable avoidance, you strengthen that muscle. Every time you move forward without waiting for motivation to catch up, you expand your capacity to grow.

In that process, I discovered that my deepest values weren't the ones handed to me by society, family, or cultural programming. They rose up from alignment with love, truth, and the woman I was consciously becoming through daily choices.

What I once viewed as flaws or failures eventually revealed themselves as the very experiences that equipped me to lead and teach. They gave me insight, empathy, and credibility I couldn't have gained any other way.

My healing wasn't just evidence for myself—it became evidence that change is available to anyone willing to do the work. The capacity to grow isn't something you go out and find; it's already built into you, waiting to be developed through steady practice and intentional choice.

Wisdom As Identity

True wisdom isn't about knowing everything—it's about knowing how to live what you've learned. It's not the accumulation of lessons, but the integration of them into who you are and how you show up.

Wisdom shows itself in the way you pause before reacting, in the boundaries you hold with quiet confidence, in the compassion you extend even while telling the truth. It's less about the words you speak and more about the steadiness you embody.

What makes wisdom powerful is that it's practical. It's found in nervous system regulation, in learning to return yourself to calm. It's found in body awareness, in choosing nourishment over punishment. It's found in spirit, in trusting that you don't have to control every outcome in order to move forward.

Wisdom is also cyclical. It asks you to return again and again to the same practices—reflection, honesty, recalibration—because growth isn't linear. With each cycle, you move a little deeper into alignment, a little stronger in your convictions, a little clearer about what really matters.

And wisdom is generous. Once it's integrated, it naturally spills over into how you guide others. You don't need to announce it or prove it—people feel it in your presence. Your scars become maps. Your lessons become light. Your steady steps make the path easier for the ones coming behind you.

The invitation at the end of this journey is simple: stop chasing wisdom as if it's somewhere out there to earn, and start living it as who you already are becoming. Let your body, mind, and spirit remind you daily: you are not broken. You are becoming. You are whole.

Wisdom isn't a finish line—it's an identity. And the more you live it, the more it teaches the world around you what is possible.

CHAPTER CHECKPOINT: THE WISDOM INTEGRATION ACTIVATION

Part 1: Authentic Self Assessment (15 minutes)

- List 5 qualities you've been told are "too much" or "too intense"
- Reframe each quality as a strength and gift rather than a flaw
- Choose one quality to express more fully in your daily life
- Plan specific ways to honor this aspect of yourself this week

Part 2: Purpose Discovery Process (20 minutes)

- Write about your three most difficult life experiences
- For each experience, identify 3 ways it made you stronger, wiser, or more compassionate
- Describe how you could use each lesson to help someone else
- Commit to one specific action that transforms your pain into someone else's hope

Part 3: Life Design Experiment (20 minutes)

- Identify one element of your ideal life you could test on a small scale
- Design a 7-day experiment to try this element
- Define what success would look like for this experiment
- Schedule the experiment into your calendar with specific actions

Part 4: Power Reclamation Practice (15 minutes)

- Identify 3 situations where you typically shrink to make others comfortable
- For each situation, write a response that honors your authentic self
- Practice expressing your power without apology in one low-stakes situation
- Plan how you'll gradually expand this authentic expression

Part 5: Success Redefinition Exercise (15 minutes)

- Write your old definition of success (external achievements, approval, etc.)
- Write your new definition of success (alignment, fulfillment, contribution)
- Identify one area where you're still chasing old success metrics
- Make one decision that aligns with your authentic success definition

YOUR WISDOM EMBODIMENT WORKSHEET

Wisdom is the integration of everything you've learned through growth, love, and overcoming. When old doubts or limiting patterns try to resurface, use this toolkit to remember who you've become and what you now know to be true.

When You Question Your Worth:

1. I am valuable because:

   ____

2. Evidence of my growth and strength:

   a) I used to ________________, now I ________________

   b) I used to ________________, now I ________________

   c) I used to ________________, now I ________________

3. My unique gifts and contributions are:

   ____

When Others Try to Dim Your Light:

1. I will not apologize for:

   ____

2. My power serves others by:

   ____

3. When someone calls me "too much," I remember:

   ____

4. The people who celebrate my authentic self are:

   ____

When You Feel Lost or Confused:

1. My core values are:

   ____

2. I make decisions by asking:

   ____

3. My life purpose connects to:

   ____

4. The legacy I'm creating is:

   ____

When You Want to Quit or Go Backward:

1. I've already overcome:

   ____

2. My pain has become purpose through:

   ____

3. The people counting on my continued growth:

   ____

4. I am becoming:

   ____

PART THREE:
GLOW ANYWAY — LIVING YOUR NEW LIFE OUT LOUD

You made it through the darkness. You learned the method. You know who you're becoming.

Now what?

Now comes the part nobody talks about in the transformation books. The part that happens after you've done the work, broken the patterns, and started to trust yourself again. The part where you have to actually live in the world with your new way of being.

This is where most people stumble. Not because they don't know how to heal, but because they don't know how to live healed.

When I was deep in my recovery, I thought the hard part was getting sober. Facing my trauma. Learning to set boundaries. Breaking the cycles that had been running my family for generations.

I was wrong.

The hard part was waking up every day and choosing to live as the woman I was becoming instead of the woman I used to be. The hard part was showing up authentically when people expected the old version of me. The hard part was refusing to shrink back down when my growth made others uncomfortable.

The hard part was learning to glow anyway.

Not when conditions were perfect. Not when everyone understood. Not when the path was clear and the outcome was guaranteed.

Right in the middle of real life. Real problems. Real setbacks. Real people who didn't always celebrate the new me.

That's what Part Three is about. It's about what happens when you stop hiding and start living out loud. When you stop waiting for permission and start giving it to yourself. When you stop surviving your days and start designing them.

But let's be honest about something. Living your new life doesn't mean you'll never fall back into old patterns. It doesn't mean you'll never have moments of doubt, days when the old voices get loud, or seasons when everything feels hard again.

It means you'll know how to get back up when you fall. It means you'll speak to yourself with kindness instead of cruelty when you stumble. It means you'll remember that a setback doesn't erase your progress—it just means you're human.

The glow you've been building throughout this book? It's not fragile. It's not dependent on perfect circumstances or flawless execution. It's not something that disappears the moment life gets messy.

Your glow is unshakable because it comes from within. It's built on truth, not pretense. It's rooted in self-respect, not external validation. It's powered by purpose, not perfection.

In the next three chapters, we're going to talk about what it really looks like to live as this new version of yourself. We'll cover how to design days you don't want to escape from, how to handle the inevitable moments when old patterns try to resurface, and what it means to keep glowing even when life doesn't cooperate with your plans.

You'll learn that building a life you love is an ongoing practice, not a one-time achievement. That resistance and setbacks are part of the process, not evidence that you're failing. That living authentically requires courage every single day, but that courage gets easier the more you practice it.

Most importantly, you'll discover that your story doesn't end when you finish this book. It begins.

Because everything you've learned, every pattern you've broken, every time you've chosen yourself over settling—it's all been a preparation for this moment. The moment you stop just surviving and start truly living.

Your transformation was never meant to be kept private. Your healing was never meant to be hidden. Your growth was never supposed to make you smaller.

You were meant to live out loud. To take up space. To let your light shine so brightly that others can see what's possible for themselves.

The world needs people who have done the work and aren't afraid to show the scars. People who have fallen down and gotten back up and are willing to teach others how to do the same. People who understand that glowing anyway doesn't mean pretending everything is perfect—it means being real about what it takes to build a life worth living.

That's you now. You're the woman who faced her demons and chose healing. You're the person who broke generational patterns and decided the cycle stops here. You're the one who learned to love yourself enough to demand better.

Now it's time to live like it.

Not someday when you have it all figured out. Not when the fear goes away completely. Not when everyone around you understands and supports your growth.

Now. Today. In the messy, imperfect, beautifully complicated life you're building one choice at a time.

Your old life is cancelled. Your new life is waiting.

Let's go live it out loud.

Chapter 8: Building a Life You Don't Want to Escape From

I'll never forget the first morning I woke up back in Phoenix at my auntie's house after leaving the chaos.

She didn't really have space for me, but she still welcomed me without asking for anything in return. For three months, I slept in a quiet corner of her pool room on a camping cot, grateful for the chance to begin again while I saved enough money to get an apartment of my own.

The silence didn't scare me anymore. It whispered possibility.

For years, I'd been waking up with dread pooling in my stomach before my feet hit the floor—the weight of another day I had to survive instead of live, another eighteen hours of pretending I was fine while slowly dying inside.

But this morning was different. I opened my eyes and felt something I hadn't experienced in years: curiosity about what the day might hold.

I made my bed intentionally, not frantically. I brewed coffee slowly, tasting it instead of chugging it. I stood at the kitchen window watching the sun come up, and for the first time in forever, I wasn't plotting an escape route from my own life.

I was designing it.

That's when it hit me like lightning: I wasn't just escaping my old life anymore. I was building a new one. And the architect of this new life was me.

The woman who used to wake up defeated was learning to wake up deliberately. The woman who used to dread her days was learning to design them.

That morning, I discovered the difference between surviving your life and creating it.

Permission to Want More

Growing up, I learned that wanting more meant you were ungrateful. Selfish. Greedy.
"Be thankful for what you have," they said.
"Some people have it worse," they reminded me.
"You should be grateful," they insisted.

As if gratitude and desire couldn't coexist in the same heart.

So I learned to swallow dreams before they even left my lips. I learned to make do, to settle, to play the good girl who never reached too far. I became an expert at convincing myself that whatever crumbs I was given were enough.

I'll never forget the first time I finally bet on myself. I invested in a mastermind I knew would help me grow. The cost was significant, and to cover most of it, I cleared out a TSP account.

By the time this opportunity came around, I had already asked for a divorce. But because we were still legally married, my ex had to sign off on me taking the money out. He didn't say anything at the time—he couldn't—but it came back up later in the divorce.

"You're being irresponsible."
"Wasting money on fantasies."

He had no faith in me. But I did.

I saw what he couldn't see.

And that became the turning point. I realized the very thing I was being shamed for—wanting more—was the very thing that was going to save me.

Daily Permission Practice

Now, giving myself permission is an everyday practice.

Sometimes it's choosing rest instead of running myself into the ground to prove my worth.
Sometimes it's saying no when I used to automatically say yes to keep the peace.
Sometimes it's allowing myself to dream bigger than my current reality without apologizing for the space those dreams require.

Permission doesn't cancel gratitude. I'm thankful for where I am, but I refuse to confuse "thankful" with "settle." Wanting more is how I honor the life God gave me. It's how I show my daughters that being grateful and reaching higher can exist in the same breath.

One of my clients, Sarah, came to me completely burnt out from her corporate job. She felt guilty for wanting to leave because, as she said, "I should be grateful to have a good paying job." We worked together to reframe that belief. She learned that gratitude for the stability the job provided could coexist with her desire for work that aligned with her values.

Six months later, she started her own consulting business. She tells me now that giving herself permission to want more didn't make her ungrateful—it made her brave.

The Architecture of Intentional Living

For most of my life, I was hoping things would get better instead of designing them to be better.

I hoped tomorrow I'd wake up with motivation. I hoped circumstances would align. I hoped other people would change. I hoped life would somehow fall into place if I just waited long enough.

But hope without action becomes wishful thinking. And wishful thinking nearly cost me my life.

Hope waits. Design creates.

I learned this through pain—what it feels like to live days you want to run away from. Checking out every night, dreading every morning, losing myself in the space between who I was and who I thought I should be.

That pain became my teacher. It showed me exactly what I never wanted to return to. When you reverse engineer your end result and design the patterns to match, your life stops being random. You become the architect. You become the woman of the future you would be proud of.

The question that changed everything for me was simple: "Who is she?" Not who do I want to be someday, but who is the woman I'm becoming right now? How does she walk into a room? How does she treat her body? How does she speak to her children? What kind of love surrounds her?

I could see her clearly. Future me was unshakable. She was proud of the road she'd walked. She wasn't afraid to show her scars or ashamed of the times she'd fallen. She was respected because she respected herself first.

Here's what I realized: I didn't have to wait years to become her. I could embody her now. I could dress like her, speak like her, love like her. That's how you manifest the woman you're becoming—you start living as her today.

The Three Pillars of Intentional Design

Building a life you don't want to escape from requires three foundational pillars:

Pillar 1: Awareness

First, you have to face the truth about your autopilot patterns. For years, I told myself I was fine. That if I just kept my head down and pushed through, things would eventually get better.

Awareness means you stop lying to yourself about what's working and what's not. You stop pretending the drinking doesn't control you. You stop convincing yourself that stress is just temporary. You stop accepting exhaustion as normal.

You can't change what you're still pretending not to see. And I pretended for a long time. That pretending kept me stuck in a life I didn't want for myself.

The Autopilot Audit I do with my clients is simple but powerful: For one week, write down every choice you make without thinking. What you eat, how you respond to stress, what you do when you get home from work, how you speak to yourself.

Most people are shocked to discover how much of their life they're living unconsciously. How many decisions they're making from old programming instead of current values.

Pillar 2: Reprogramming

This was the hardest and most beautiful part of my journey. I had to rewire my subconscious mind—the part of me that expected pain, that was always bracing for chaos, that believed love had to be earned.

I had to teach my mind to filter life through love instead of fear. Abundance instead of scarcity. Possibility instead of limitation.

It didn't happen overnight. It was daily work. It was catching the old voice that whispered hateful things and refusing to let it run the show. At first, it felt awkward—like trying to speak a language I didn't know. But repetition creates truth. The more I practiced self-compassion, the more my brain began to believe me.

Slowly, love became the new lens I saw the world through.

Pillar 3: Intentional Design

Once you know where you're headed, you start building your days to match it. That's where the real shift happens.

Morning and evening routines that ground you instead of rush you. Boundaries that protect your energy instead of drain it. Even the way you speak to yourself becomes part of the design.

Ordinary moments take on new meaning. A cup of coffee becomes a pause to ground yourself instead of just caffeine to survive the day. Getting dressed becomes an act of showing up for the woman you're becoming instead of just covering your body. Conversations with yourself transform from harsh critiques to gentle reminders of who you're growing into.

When you build your life this way—piece by piece, choice by choice—you stop living a life you want to escape from. You create a life you can't stop smiling about because every part of it reflects who you've decided to be.

The Perfect Day Blueprint

Let me walk you through what a perfect day looks like in my new life. Not perfect because everything goes smoothly, but perfect because I feel grounded while moving through it.

I wake up before the house stirs. Not to race against the clock, but to actually be with myself. I move my body—sometimes it's a full workout, sometimes it's just stretching on my bedroom floor. I breathe. I center myself. I sip my coffee in silence before anyone needs me.

When my six-year-old gets up for school, I'm present. I'm not barking orders, rushing around, or already stressed about the day ahead. I can smile at her bedhead, listen to her little stories about her dreams, and send her off to school with her feeling seen instead of hurried.

With my three-year-old at home, the rhythm is slower but still intentional. We play, read, run errands together. I weave in time to build my business, but I don't let work swallow our moments of connection.

I'm heavily goal-oriented, so I plan my days with strategy the night before. I block out time, set priorities, and make sure my to-do list lines up with the bigger vision I'm building. But I don't let structure squeeze the joy out of my day.

There's a balance—I maximize my efforts and make sure we're having fun in the process. Whether I'm working, playing, or cleaning, I find ways to make it the happiest time possible.

The difference between my old days and my new days comes down to one thing: intention. I'm no longer reacting to life. I'm responding to it. I'm no longer surviving my days. I'm designing them.

Creating Your Perfect Day

Here's how you design yours:

Start with how you want to feel at the end of the day. Accomplished? Peaceful? Connected? Energized? Work backward from that feeling.

What would need to happen during your day for you to feel that way? What morning routine would set you up for success? What boundaries would protect your energy? What evening practice would help you wind down with gratitude instead of exhaustion?

Don't try to overhaul everything at once. Pick one element—maybe your morning routine—and perfect that first. Once it becomes automatic, add another piece.

Remember: You're not trying to create a schedule so rigid it breaks when life happens. You're creating a framework flexible enough to bend without breaking.

From Survival Mode to Thriving Mode

There's a specific feeling that comes with survival mode, and if you've been there, you know exactly what I'm talking about.

You wake up already behind. The day feels like something to get through instead of something to experience. You're constantly putting out fires, reacting to crises, running on fumes.

You check out at night because consciousness feels too heavy. You dread mornings because they represent another day of the same struggle. You live for weekends, vacations, any escape from the reality you've created.

You make decisions from fear instead of love. You choose what's safe over what's aligned. You survive instead of thrive.

What Changes in Thriving Mode

When you shift from survival to thriving, everything changes—but it's often subtle at first.

Energy returns because you're no longer constantly fighting yourself. Decision-making becomes clearer because you're operating from your values instead of your fears. Time feels more spacious because you're present instead of always thinking about what's next.

You stop needing weekends to recover from your life and start looking forward to Mondays because your days feel meaningful.

Thriving mode means you're no longer asking, *"How do I get through this?"* You're asking, *"How do I grow through this?"*

And the first shift isn't usually external—it's internal. Instead of trying to do everything perfectly, you start focusing on doing the right things consistently. Instead of reacting to every problem like a crisis, you learn to respond from your priorities.

From there, everything else begins to feel different—work becomes more manageable, relationships more fulfilling, and there's finally energy left for what matters most.

The shift from survival to thriving doesn't require a complete life overhaul. It requires a complete perspective overhaul.

Creating Your Daily Rhythm

The difference between routine and rhythm is flexibility. Routines are rigid and break when life gets complicated. Rhythms are fluid and adapt to what each day requires.

My morning rhythm includes movement, stillness, and nourishment—but what those look like depends on the day. Sometimes movement is a full workout, sometimes it's five minutes of stretching. Sometimes stillness is twenty minutes of meditation, sometimes it's three deep breaths before my feet hit the floor.

The point is consistency of intention, not consistency of action.

Your rhythm should include anchors that ground your day and flexibility that allows for life to happen. Think of it as creating a framework that supports you instead of confines you.

The Standards That Save You

Here's something I learned the hard way: When you lower your standards, you lower your life.

I spent years accepting crumbs and convincing myself they were a meal. I let people treat me poorly because I thought that's what I deserved. I lowered my expectations to match my low self-worth.

That almost killed me.

Every time you compromise your values, you chip away at your self-respect. Every time you accept less than you deserve, you reinforce the belief that you're not worth more.

I stayed in relationships that drained me because I was afraid of being alone. I took jobs that bored me because I was afraid of taking risks. I shrunk to avoid conflict because I was afraid of being too much.

But playing small to make others comfortable was slowly suffocating my soul.

The day I decided to honor my worth instead of hide from it, everything changed. I started setting standards that protected the woman I was becoming instead of enabling the woman I'd been.

My Non-Negotiable Guardrails

Here are the standards I'll never compromise again:

Peace comes first. My home, my relationships, my mind—peace is non-negotiable. If something or someone consistently disrupts my peace, it gets examined, adjusted, or removed.

My daughters get the best of me, not what's left of me. I organize my energy around what matters most. They don't get my exhausted, depleted, distracted version. They get my presence, my attention, my joy.

I don't beg for love, attention, or respect. If it's not given freely, it doesn't belong to me. I don't chase, convince, or perform for affection. I attract what matches my energy.

I don't numb myself to get through life. I choose to feel everything—the hard emotions and the beautiful ones. I face my life instead of escaping from it.

I don't play small with my dreams. My goals matter. My vision matters. I refuse to apologize for wanting more or shrink my dreams to fit other people's comfort zones.

These guardrails protect the woman I've worked so hard to become. They're not rules—they're acts of self-respect.

Setting Your Own Standards

What standards do you need to set to protect your peace? What boundaries do you need to honor your worth? What non-negotiables do you need to establish to honor your growth?

Write them down. Make them specific. Then live by them, even when it's uncomfortable.

Remember: Standards aren't about perfection. They're about protection. They protect your energy, your peace, your progress, and your purpose.

A Life You Can't Stop Smiling About

There's a difference between happiness and alignment, and understanding that difference changed everything for me.

Happiness is a mood. It comes and goes based on circumstances. Alignment is a lifestyle. It comes from living in harmony with your values regardless of what's happening around you.

For years, I chased happiness. I thought if I could just get the right job, the right relationship, the right body, the right bank account, then I'd be happy.

But happiness built on external circumstances is fragile. It disappears the moment circumstances change.

The Undercurrent of Joy

When you live aligned with your values, you create an undercurrent of joy that isn't dependent on perfect conditions. You stop needing life to be perfect to feel peace.

I wasn't just chasing "happy" anymore—I was building a life I didn't want to escape from. That's when my smile stopped leaving my face, because it wasn't tied to circumstances. It wasn't coming from outside of me. It was rising from within.

The shift happened when I stopped asking "What will make me happy?" and started asking "What will make me proud of myself?"

Pride builds differently than happiness. Pride comes from integrity, from keeping promises to yourself, from choosing growth over comfort, from living aligned with your values even when it's hard.

Building Joy Into Ordinary Moments

Joy doesn't require grand gestures or perfect circumstances. Joy can be found in a Tuesday morning cup of coffee when you're fully present to taste it. Joy can be found in folding laundry when you're grateful for clothes to wear and a family to care for.

Joy can be found in the decision to speak kindly to yourself instead of critically. Joy can be found in choosing to see beauty instead of focusing on what's broken.

The woman I was before needed external validation to feel good about herself. The woman I am now generates validation from the inside out. She creates joy in ordinary moments because she's learned that joy is a choice, not a circumstance.

Living Out Loud

I don't hide anymore because I don't have time to. I've got things to do. I've got a testimony that needs to be told. I've got women to help who are where I once was.

Fear used to paralyze me—fear of judgment, fear of failure, fear of being too much. But fear doesn't get to run my life anymore. I've already lost too much time to it.

Visibility stopped being about being liked. It became about being useful. I tell my story not to impress anyone, but to teach. To show another woman that she can rebuild too. To prove that you don't have to have it all together to stand tall.

When you live out loud, you give other people permission to stop hiding too. That's how cycles break. That's how healing spreads. That's how the world changes—one woman at a time deciding she's worthy of the life she wants.

Teaching Your Children to Glow

Every choice I make now, I make with my daughters in mind. Not in a way that puts pressure on me to be perfect, but in a way that reminds me of the legacy I'm creating.

What am I teaching them about a woman's worth through how I treat myself? What am I showing them about resilience through how I handle challenges? What am I modeling about love through how I care for my own heart?

I want them to see a woman who honors herself. Who sets boundaries. Who chooses growth over comfort. Who glows not because her life is perfect, but because she refuses to let imperfection dim her light.

I want them to inherit a lineage of women who know their worth. Who speak their truth. Who take up space without apology. Who break cycles instead of repeating them.

The work I do on myself is for every woman who comes after me. It's for the daughters I'm raising and the daughters they might raise someday.

This is how generational healing works. One woman at a time. One choice at a time. One glow at a time.

Your New Beginning

You now have the blueprint for creating a life you don't want to escape from. You have permission to want more. You understand the difference between hoping and designing. You know how to create daily rhythms that support your growth.

Most importantly, you know that you are the architect of your own experience.

The woman you're becoming doesn't wait for perfect conditions to live fully. She doesn't postpone joy until everything aligns. She doesn't need external permission to honor her worth.

She moves through her days with intention. She sets standards that guard her peace. She shapes an environment that reflects her values and supports her vision.

She thrives because her life rests on alignment, not perfection—on choices that honor her truth, not the expectations of others.

That woman is you. She's been waiting for you to claim her. She's been waiting for you to trust her. She's been waiting for you to give her space to lead.

The blueprint is yours. The permission is granted. The tools are already in your hands.

Now go live a life so meaningful, so aligned, and so deeply yours that you never want to escape from it.

Chapter 9:
Relapse & Resistance

There's a picture on my phone from August 2023. I'm in the best shape of my life—muscles defined, skin glistening, striking a pose for Leilani, my photographer, right after a workout. Strong. Disciplined. Proud.

Six months later, I could barely recognize that woman.

By spring 2024, I was working 15–18 hour shifts at a gas station with no days off, running on energy drinks and slices of convenience-store pizza, watching the muscle I had fought so hard for fade in the mirror. The woman who once meal-prepped and fueled herself with fresh fruits and vegetables was now grabbing whatever wouldn't spoil in her car. The woman who never missed a workout was too exhausted to even think about stepping into the gym.

I had backslid hard.

Not into drinking. Not into the old destructive patterns that nearly killed me. But into survival mode—into letting the demands of the day dictate my choices instead of my values, into believing that just getting through each day was enough.

And for the first time in years, I had to face a truth that every person on a healing journey eventually confronts: you can do everything right and still fall backward.

This chapter isn't about perfection. It's about the messy middle of transformation. The part where you slip, stumble, and sometimes crash completely. The part where resistance shows up not as proof you're failing, but as evidence you're stretching beyond your old comfort zone.

And it's in that space that the real lesson emerges: setbacks are not the opposite of growth—they're part of it. Falling doesn't erase the work you've done. It teaches you resilience. It strengthens your capacity. It shows you how to keep moving forward with new awareness.

Because falling down doesn't mean you're broken. Learning how to rise again—over and over—is what makes you unstoppable.

The Myth of Linear Healing

Let me tell you what nobody puts in the transformation stories: Healing looks like a drunk person walking home. Lots of side steps, a few stumbles, occasionally walking backward before finally making it to the front door.

We're sold this fantasy that once you "do the work," you're done. Once you have your breakthrough moment, identify your patterns, and commit to change, you graduate into some permanent state of enlightenment where old behaviors can't touch you anymore.

That's not healing. That's a fairy tale.

Real healing is cyclical. It spirals. You revisit the same lessons at deeper levels. You think you've mastered something, only to discover there's another layer waiting for you.

I spent years believing that if I slipped back into an old pattern, it meant I was broken. That all my growth was fake. That I was destined to repeat the same cycles forever.

But here's what I learned in those gas station parking lots, eating cold pizza at 2 a.m. because I was too tired to cook: Relapse isn't proof that you're failing. It's proof that you're human.

The difference between who I was before and who I am now isn't that I don't fall. It's how quickly I get back up.

When Life Knocked Me Sideways

Let me take you back to that season when everything I'd built started crumbling.

November 2023: I left the family house with a ten-foot U-Haul towing my car with barely enough in savings to make the move. I didn't bring my girls—I asked their father to keep them while I got back on my feet, and I would come back for them. He agreed. What I didn't know then was how quickly that arrangement would become another source of stress in the divorce.

The home workouts I'd done faithfully in my garage were no longer part of my reality when my days began at 3 a.m. to start a 15-hour shift. The fresh fruits and vegetables I used to fill my body with were out of reach on my budget. The morning routine that once grounded me became impossible when exhaustion was the only thing waiting for me at the start of the day.

I told myself it was temporary—that once stability returned, I'd go back to the habits that made me feel like myself. But weeks turned into months, and the temporary started to feel permanent.

The woman who used to wake up before her alarm was hitting snooze five times. The woman who was living on whatever the gas station stocked. The woman who never missed a workout was falling asleep in her office.

I watched my reflection change—not just my body, but my eyes. The light I'd worked so hard to reignite was dimming again.

And the voice started up. You know the one—the voice that had been quiet for so long I'd almost forgotten it existed:

See? You can't maintain this. You're just pretending to be someone you're not. This is who you really are. This is where you belong.

The Whisper That Nearly Won

Resistance doesn't kick down your front door. It slips in through the back, quiet as smoke.

It whispers things like:

- "You're tired. Skip the workout. You've done enough already."
- "One fast food meal won't matter. You deserve something easy."
- "You don't have time for self-care right now. Maybe when things calm down."
- "This is just how life is. Stop trying to be something you're not."

For months, I let those whispers drag me into long arguments with myself. I'd justify, debate, negotiate. By the time I was done, I was exhausted and the whisper had won.

That's how resistance works. Not by force, but by wearing you down. Making the old way seem reasonable. Making growth feel like a luxury you can't afford.

I'd catch myself in the gas station bathroom mirror, uniform wrinkled, hair falling out of its ponytail, and think: *Maybe this is just who I am. Maybe I was fooling myself thinking I could be someone different.*

The woman who used to run every choice through the filter of "Does this move me closer to who I'm becoming?" was running choices through "What's the easiest thing I can do right now?"

And for a while, that voice was winning.

The Spiral I Used to Know

Here's what would have happened to the old me in this situation:

I would have interpreted the backslide as proof that I was fundamentally flawed. I would have used it as evidence that change was impossible for someone like me. I would have poured all my shame into a bottle and numbed myself into forgetting that I ever tried to be better.

The spiral would have looked like this:

- Miss one workout → "I'm lazy"
- Eat one unhealthy meal → "I have no self-control"
- Skip one self-care practice → "I'm not worth the effort"
- Make one choice from fear instead of love → "I'm broken"

Each slip would have been ammunition against myself. Proof that I should stop trying. Evidence that the woman I'd been becoming was just an act I couldn't maintain.

I would have stayed down for months. Maybe years.

But something was different this time. Even in the middle of the backslide, even when I felt like I was losing myself again, I had something I'd never had before: Tools.

The Tools That Saved Me

The woman pulling 16-hour shifts looked different from the one who used to drown her nights in Jack Daniel's. She carried lessons now—habits and hard-won resilience that held up even when everything else was falling apart.

When the gym was out of reach, I did push-ups on the living room floor. When organic wasn't in the budget, I chose protein over chips when I could. When my full morning ritual was impossible, I still took five minutes to breathe before the day swallowed me whole. Small, stubborn things. Tiny commitments that stitched me back together when life tried to unravel me.

I had learned the difference between slipping and quitting. Between having a bad day and abandoning everything I'd worked for.

Most importantly, I had learned to be compassionate with myself when I fell short.

The voice that used to say *"You're worthless"* had been replaced with *"You're learning."*

The voice that used to say *"You ruined everything"* had been replaced with *"Tomorrow is a chance to try again."*

The voice that used to say *"Why even bother?"* had been replaced with *"Because you're worth fighting for."*

My Comeback Protocol

Now when I catch myself falling back into old patterns, I don't let it swallow me whole. I have a protocol. A way back to myself that doesn't require perfection, just willingness.

Step 1: Pause and Name It

No exaggerating. No dramatizing. Just the facts.

"I slipped." "I made a choice from fear instead of love." "I'm off track."

Owning it quickly keeps it from ballooning into something bigger than it is. The faster you can name what's happening without judgment, the faster you can redirect.

Step 2: Interrupt the Spiral

I do something small that breaks the pattern. Drink a glass of water. Step outside for two minutes. Tidy one space. Stretch my body. Text someone who believes in me.

It doesn't fix everything, but it reminds me that I'm not stuck. That I can make a different choice right now. That the next decision doesn't have to match the last one.

Step 3: Reframe the Story

Instead of *"I'm back at square one,"* I tell myself:

- "This is feedback, not failure."

- "I've done hard things before and I can get back on track."
- "Slipping doesn't erase my growth."
- "The woman I'm becoming doesn't quit because of one bad day."

The story you tell yourself about the slip matters more than the slip itself. If your inner voice is cruel, you'll stay stuck. If your inner voice is kind, you'll find your way home.

Step 4: Start Small

I don't punish myself with a ten-step recovery plan. I don't commit to overhauling my entire life by Monday. I just take one aligned action.

Cook one real meal. Show up for one workout. Honor one boundary. Make one choice that the woman I'm becoming would make.

One win leads to another. Then another. Then another.

Step 5: Remember My Why

I remind myself why I started this journey in the first place. I think about my daughters watching me. I think about the woman I was in that 2 a.m. moment with the gun in my hands. I think about all the other women who need to see that change is possible.

I remember that my healing isn't just for me. It's for every woman who's been told she's too broken to change. It's for my daughters who will inherit whatever patterns I choose to break or repeat.

That bigger purpose gives me strength when my own motivation fails.

The Difference Between a Setback and a Breakdown

A setback and a breakdown might look the same from the outside, but they feel different in your body.

A **setback** is surface level. You're still connected to your core self, still operating from your values, just struggling with execution. You know who you are and where you're going. You're just having trouble getting there today.

A **breakdown** goes deeper. It's when you lose connection to yourself entirely. When you forget why you started. When the path forward disappears and you can't remember what you were fighting for.

Setbacks require compassion and redirection. Breakdowns require rest and professional support.

Learning to tell the difference has been crucial for my mental health. When I'm having a setback, I can implement my comeback protocol and trust that I'll find my way back. When I'm moving toward a breakdown, I know to slow down, reach out, and get the support I need.

The gas station season was a setback, not a breakdown. I was still me underneath the exhaustion. I still knew what I valued and who I was becoming. I just needed time and grace to reconnect with those things.

When Resistance Gets Sneaky

Resistance evolves as you do. It learns your patterns and adapts its approach.

When I first started my healing journey, resistance was obvious. It told me I was worthless, that change was impossible, that I should just give up and drink.

Now that I'm stronger, resistance has gotten sneakier. It sounds reasonable. Practical. Even caring.

Modern resistance whispers:

- "You're doing so well, you can afford to slack off a little."
- "You've been so disciplined, you deserve a break."
- "One exception won't hurt anything."
- "You're being too hard on yourself."
- "Life is short, you should enjoy it more."

See how much harder this is to argue with? It's not telling you you're worthless. It's telling you you're doing great and should relax your standards.

But I've learned that the moment I start negotiating with resistance, I've already lost. The moment I engage in the internal debate about whether this one choice matters, I'm giving resistance power.

Now I run every choice through a simple filter: Does this move me closer to the woman I'm becoming, or further away?

If closer, I do it. If further away, I don't. No drama. No shame spiral. Just a decision, and then I move on.

Most of the time, I already know what the answer should be. Which means I've had to raise my tolerance for discomfort. I tell myself "no" to the easy option more often than I say "yes."

Because that's how you grow. You stack more uncomfortable yeses than easy nos.

The Shame That Used to Destroy Me

The old me didn't just fall off track. I fell into shame.

Shame was always heavier than the relapse itself. The mistake was never what destroyed me. It was the story I told myself about the mistake. The weeks and months I spent ruminating, replaying, punishing myself.

"You ruined everything." "You'll never get it right." "Why even bother trying?"

That internal dialogue cost me more time than any actual setback ever did.

Here's what I know now that I wish I'd known then: The slip isn't the enemy. The shame is.

Shame is what keeps you down long after you could have gotten back up. Shame is what turns a temporary setback into a permanent identity. Shame is what makes you forget that you're still worthy of love, still capable of growth, still deserving of your own compassion.

Now, when I slip, I feel disappointment. Sometimes frustration. But I don't feel ashamed.

Because I know that slipping doesn't make me a failure. It makes me human.

The Gift Hidden in the Fall

Looking back on that gas station season, I can see gifts that weren't visible at the time.

I learned that my worth isn't tied to my performance. That I can love myself even when I'm not operating at peak capacity. That the woman I'm becoming doesn't disappear when life gets hard. She just adapts.

I learned that muscle memory is real. Not just physical muscle memory, but emotional and spiritual muscle memory. When I returned to the gym months later, my body remembered how to move. When I returned to my self-care practices, my spirit remembered how to glow.

I learned that starting again doesn't mean starting from zero. It means starting with experience. With knowledge. With proof that I've climbed this mountain before.

Maybe that's the real lesson. When life knocks you off track, you don't go back to square one. You go back with wisdom. You go back with evidence that you're capable of hard things. You go back with compassion for the woman who fell and respect for the woman who got back up.

The Comeback That Counted

My comeback didn't start with some perfect plan. It didn't begin with a dramatic moment of inspiration or a life-changing epiphany.

It started with basics: water instead of energy drinks. A ten-minute walk outside instead of convincing myself it had to be an hour at the gym. One phone call to a friend instead of isolating. One moment of kindness toward myself instead of criticism.

Simple things stacked over time. Each small win was proof that I was moving forward again. Each aligned choice was evidence that the woman I'd been becoming was still there—just waiting for me to remember her.

The difference between my old comebacks and this one was gentleness. I didn't try to punish myself back into shape. I didn't commit to unrealistic changes that would set me up for another fall.

I came back by treating myself like someone I loved who was struggling. Someone who needed encouragement, not criticism. Someone who needed support, not judgment.

I came back by remembering that progress isn't about perfection. It's about direction. And as long as I kept taking steps toward the woman I was becoming, I was winning.

What Resistance Taught Me

Every time I've faced resistance and come through it, I've emerged stronger. Not because resistance is good, but because overcoming it proves something to yourself that nothing else can.

It proves you can trust yourself to get back up. It proves your commitment is stronger than your comfort. It proves the woman you're becoming is real, not just a fantasy you've been entertaining.

Resistance is a magnifying glass on the habits that haven't fully taken root yet. The beliefs that are still fragile. The places where you still need to show yourself love.

I don't call it failure anymore when I struggle. I call it information. A chance to study myself in real time. To ask: Where did I compromise? Where do I need stronger boundaries? Where can I offer myself more compassion?

Resistance forces me to pause, to reassess, but never to quit. Every time I've stumbled, I've walked away with clearer vision, sharper tools, and deeper respect for my own resilience.

Your Turn to Rise

If you're reading this chapter in the middle of your own backslide, hear this: You are proof that change is possible. You are destined to break every toxic pattern.

You are a human being having a human experience. You are someone brave enough to try, which already sets you apart from most people.

The fact that you fell doesn't erase the ground you've covered. The fact that you're struggling doesn't negate your growth. The fact that you're not perfect doesn't make you a failure.

It makes you real.

Here's what I want you to do right now, wherever you are in your journey:

Forgive yourself for being human. For making choices from fear instead of love. For forgetting who you were becoming. For letting circumstances dictate your decisions. Forgiveness doesn't excuse the behavior. It frees you to choose differently moving forward.

Take one small step toward the person you're becoming. Not ten steps. Not a complete life overhaul. One step. Drink a glass of water. Take three deep breaths. Send yourself one kind thought. Call one person who believes in you.

Remember your why. Why did you start this journey? What were you trying to escape from? What were you moving toward? Who is counting on you to keep going? Let that bigger purpose fuel you when your personal motivation fails.

Trust the process. Growth isn't linear. Healing isn't neat. Transformation isn't a one-time event you graduate from. It's a lifelong practice of choosing yourself again and again, especially when it's hard.

You've survived everything that's brought you to this point. You can survive this too. Not just survive it—learn from it, grow through it, and use it to become even more resilient than you were before.

The woman you're becoming doesn't quit because of one bad day. She doesn't abandon herself because of one mistake. She doesn't let temporary circumstances define her permanent identity.

She gets back up. Every single time.

That's not just who she is. That's who you are.

Chapter 10: Glow Anyway

It was a Friday morning—nothing special about the day. I was getting ready for work, rushing around my apartment, when I caught my reflection in the bedroom mirror.

And I froze.

The woman looking back at me had something I hadn't seen in years. Her shoulders were back, not hunched in defeat. Her eyes were clear, not clouded with shame. Even the way she stood—steady, rooted—carried a quiet kind of power I hadn't seen in so long.

"Who are you?" I whispered to my reflection.

The glow showed up in small ways first. Clothes fitting differently. Energy returning. The mirror slowly shifting from something I avoided to something that surprised me. It wasn't about the scale or the size tags. It was about the reminder that I could change.

But this morning was different. This wasn't just physical transformation.

The woman in the mirror looked both familiar and brand new. She stood taller, carried more weight in her presence, and for the first time in years, she looked like she truly believed in herself.

Someone who was glowing from the inside out.

And then it hit me: this is what it looks like to refuse to let your circumstances define your spirit.

This is what it means to glow anyway.

What It Really Means to Glow When Life Isn't Perfect

Let me be clear about something: Glowing anyway isn't a hashtag you throw under a filtered selfie.

This isn't about pretending everything is fine when it's not. It's not about forcing positivity over pain or slapping a smile over exhaustion and calling it resilience.

I confused glow with achievement for years. I thought if I could just get my life perfect enough, if I could just control enough variables, if I could just achieve enough goals, then I'd earn the right to feel good about myself.

That's not glow. That's conditional joy. And conditional joy is just another cage.

Real glow means you stop waiting for the conditions to line up before you let yourself live. It's refusing to postpone your happiness until the debt is paid off, until your body looks a certain way, until the relationship feels easy, until the kids are grown, until the career is stable.

Glow is presence. It's letting yourself smile in the middle of mayhem. Laughing in the kitchen while the laundry still waits. Breathing in the sunlight even while your heart aches. Dancing to music only you can hear while the world burns around you.

It's giving yourself permission to feel all the emotions without shame. Grief and gratitude. Frustration and hope. Anger and love. They can coexist. They do coexist. And pretending they don't is what keeps you numb.

The Difference Between Toxic Positivity and Real Glow

For years, I forced myself into toxic positivity because I thought that's what strength looked like. I told myself, "Be grateful. Be positive. Don't show weakness." I slapped motivational quotes over my exhaustion and called it healing.

It wasn't healing. It was denial.

Toxic positivity is a performance for the world. Glow is a practice for the soul.

Toxic positivity tells you to ignore the pain. Glow says to carry the pain, but don't forget the beauty.

Toxic positivity demands that you pretend everything is fine. Glow admits when things aren't fine and still chooses not to dim the light.

Toxic positivity is rigid and fragile. Glow is flexible and resilient.

Here's the difference: When I was stuck in toxic positivity, I would get angry at myself for having negative emotions. I would judge my grief, shame my anger, and push through exhaustion because I thought that's what strong people do.

Now, when grief shows up, I welcome her. I let her sit with me. I honor what she has to teach me. But I don't let her move in permanently.

When anger arrives, I don't banish her. I listen to what she's protecting. I feel her fire. I let her motivate me to create boundaries or make changes. But I don't let her poison my relationships.

When exhaustion knocks on my door, I don't ignore her. I rest. I nourish myself. I slow down. But I don't let her convince me that I'm weak or broken.

The emotions don't control me anymore. But I don't control them either. We coexist. We dance together. And somehow, in that dance, the light leaks through the cracks.

That's glow. Not the absence of darkness, but the presence of light in spite of it.

How I Maintain My Glow When Life Gets Messy

Life still gets messy. The laundry still piles up. The bills still need paying. The kids still have meltdowns. Work still brings stress. Relationships still require effort.

The difference is that I don't waste my energy trying to keep everything spotless anymore. I've learned that glow doesn't come from perfect conditions. It comes from staying rooted in myself in the middle of the disarray.

My Glow-Maintenance Toolkit

When chaos tries to dim my light, I have practices that anchor me back to myself:

Breathe before you react. This sounds simple, but it's revolutionary. Most of my old destructive patterns came from reacting instead of responding. Now, when something triggers me, I pause. I take three deep breaths. I ask myself, "What would the woman I'm becoming do here?" Usually, the answer is different from my first impulse.

Reach for water before you reach for escape. Whether it's food, alcohol, shopping, or mindless scrolling, most of us have something we reach for when we want to numb or distract ourselves. I've trained myself to drink a glass of water first. It sounds ridiculous, but it creates a pause. A moment of choice. And sometimes that's all you need to choose differently.

Move the energy through your body. When emotions get heavy, I don't sugarcoat them. If I'm angry, I let myself feel it. But I don't stay in it too long because holding it in only poisons you. I run. I scream into a pillow. I dance it out. I let it move through me and out of me. Glow doesn't come from pretending the darkness isn't there. It comes from giving it a healthy exit.

Protect your energy with boundaries. I say no when my plate is full. I step back from people who drain me. I remind myself that peace is worth more than pleasing others. Sometimes you can't walk away from people completely, but you can change how much access they have to your energy.

Ground yourself in prayer or meditation. When my mind starts to spiral, I get still. I breathe. I connect to something bigger than myself. Whether you call it God, the universe, source energy, or simply your higher self, connecting to that deeper wisdom reminds you that this moment is temporary and you are stronger than you know.

The Seasons of Glow

Here's something nobody tells you: Your glow will have seasons.

There will be times when you feel unstoppable. When everything flows. When you feel so connected to yourself that nothing can shake you. Celebrate these times. But don't get attached to them as the only definition of success.

There will be times when your glow feels dim. When life feels heavy. When you're just trying to make it through the day. This doesn't mean you're failing. This doesn't mean you've lost your progress. This means you're human.

The goal isn't to maintain peak glow at all times. The goal is to remember that your light doesn't disappear just because it's temporarily dimmed. The goal is to trust that seasons change, and this too shall pass.

Winter serves a purpose. It's when the deepest growth happens, underground where no one can see. Spring always follows. Your glow always returns. Sometimes it returns brighter than before because of what you learned in the darkness.

Why This Is a Lifelong Practice, Not a One-Time Transformation

People love transformation stories with neat beginnings, middles, and ends. The moment everything changes. The dramatic before and after. The happily ever after.

That's not how real life works.

Growth isn't a one-time transformation. It's a lifestyle. Life will always test what you've learned. Old wounds will return in new disguises. New seasons will bring fresh challenges. Just when you think you've mastered one layer, another gets revealed.

That's not a bug in the system. That's the system working exactly as it should.

Here's what I know after years of this work: The woman who can handle what you're facing today isn't the same woman who could handle what you were facing five years ago. You've grown. You've learned. You've developed new tools, new perspectives, new strengths.

But that doesn't mean you'll never face challenges again. It means you'll face them as someone different. Someone stronger. Someone who knows her worth. Someone who has tools in her toolkit. Someone who has evidence of her own resilience.

The Daily Agreements

Commitment to your growth looks like quiet rituals that steady you:

Breath before reaction. Not always, but more often than before.

Prayer before panic. Connecting to something bigger when the world feels too small.

Movement before stagnation. Getting your body involved in your healing because trauma lives in the tissues.

Nourishment before numbing. Fueling your body instead of abandoning it.

Clarity before chaos. Taking time to center yourself before diving into your day.

These aren't rules. They're sacred acts of respect for the vessel you live in. They're how you honor the woman you've fought to become.

Commitment also means self-correction. Not letting one slip pull you back into shame, but adjusting quickly. Treating setbacks as signals, not punishments. Honoring your boundaries. Protecting your peace.

Commitment is found in the quiet moments. The way you speak to yourself when no one is listening. The choices you make when no one is watching. The respect you show your own body, mind, and spirit when it would be easier to abandon yourself.

Those small moments, repeated over time, shape the woman you become.

The People Who Can't Handle Your Intensity

Let me tell you something that might sting: Not everyone will be able to handle your glow.

Some people have gotten comfortable with your dimness. They've built their identity around being the bright one, the stable one, the one who has it all together. When you start glowing, it threatens their role.

Some people are still so uncomfortable with their own darkness that your light makes them squirm. Your healing reminds them of their wounds. Your growth reminds them of their stagnation. Your joy reminds them of their resignation.

I used to think losing people meant I was doing something wrong. Maybe if I softened my voice, quieted my truth, dimmed my light, they'd stay.

But the ones who can't handle your intensity were never built for the weight of you anyway.

Here's what I know now: Your glow isn't up for negotiation.

If your light feels like too much for somebody, that's their cue to step aside, not your cue to dim it. You've paid too high a price for your radiance to apologize for it now.

The people who belong in your life don't flinch when the heat gets turned up. They lean in. They celebrate your light. They protect your glow when others try to dim it.

And the ones who walk away? Their exit just clears the path for the ones meant to walk beside you.

So live loudly. Love deeply. Glow brightly. And don't apologize for any of it.

Losing people who can't handle your growth isn't the loss you think it is. Losing yourself to keep them would be.

The Ripple Effect of Your Radiance

Here's the beautiful truth: when you glow anyway, it doesn't just change your life—it changes the room you walk into.

People feel it. Your steadiness calms their chaos. Your joy interrupts their hopelessness. Your choices give them a new reference point for what's possible.

Healing is contagious. Every time you choose presence over numbness, you expand the definition of strength for someone watching. Every time you set a boundary without apology, you remind someone else they're allowed to do the same. Every time you pursue something meaningful instead of settling, you plant the idea that they, too, can want more.

This isn't about spotlight or platform. It's about influence that happens quietly, through example: a child learning from the way you regulate your emotions, a friend reconsidering her own worth after watching you refuse to settle, a coworker daring to rest because they saw you normalize balance.

This is how cycles break: not through polished perfection, but through visible progress. Not by showing people an image of who you think you should be, but by letting them see who you truly are—healing in real time, growing in plain sight.

Your radiance is not just light for you. It's oxygen for someone else. And that's the ripple effect—your glow becomes a catalyst for transformation in lives you may never even realize you've touched.

When the Mirror Becomes Your Friend

Remember that morning when I didn't recognize my reflection? Now the mirror is one of my favorite places.

Not because I think I'm perfect. Not because I love every angle or every line. But because when I look in the mirror, I see evidence of my resilience.

I see the woman who survived the night with the gun in her hands. I see the woman who chose herself over comfortable misery. I see the woman who learned to love herself fiercely. I see the woman who turned her pain into purpose.

The lines around my eyes? Those are from laughing with my daughters. The gray hairs? Those are wisdom earned through walking through fire. The scars? Those are proof that I survived what could have killed me.

When I look in the mirror now, I don't see someone who needs fixing. I see someone who has been broken and rebuilt herself stronger. I see someone who has learned to glow not in spite of her imperfections, but because of how she's learned to love herself through them.

The mirror doesn't lie. But it also doesn't tell the whole story. What it shows you depends on what you're looking for.

If you're looking for flaws, you'll find them. If you're looking for evidence of failure, you'll see it. If you're looking for reasons to criticize yourself, they'll jump out at you.

But if you're looking for evidence of your strength, you'll see that too. If you're looking for signs of your growth, they'll be there. If you're looking for proof of your beauty, you'll find it.

The mirror reflects back what you bring to it. Bring love, and love is what you'll see.

Taking Your Power Back, Again and Again

Here's my final truth bomb, the thing I need you to never forget: This isn't a one-time event you graduate from.

Taking your power back isn't something you do once and then you're done. It's something you do again and again, every time life tries to convince you that you're powerless.

Every time someone tells you that you're too much. Every time circumstances try to dictate your worth. Every time old patterns try to reclaim you. Every time fear whispers that you should play small.

You take your power back by choosing yourself. You take your power back by honoring your truth. You take your power back by refusing to abandon yourself. You take your power back by glowing anyway.

This is not a destination. This is a way of life.

The woman you're becoming doesn't arrive somewhere and stay there. She keeps becoming. She keeps growing. She keeps choosing herself, again and again, especially when it's hard.

Your Glow Is Not Negotiable

As we close this book together, I want you to understand something: Everything you need is already inside you.

The courage you've been waiting for? It's there. The love you've been seeking? It's there. The wisdom you've been praying for? It's there. The glow you've been chasing? It's there.

You don't have to earn it. You don't have to prove you deserve it. You don't have to wait for permission from anyone else to claim it.

It has always been yours. Waiting quietly, patiently, for you to stop doubting yourself long enough to remember who you really are.

You are not missing anything. You are not behind. The life you long for doesn't begin "someday." It begins the moment you choose to believe in what's already inside you.

Your Story Starts Here

You came to this book for a reason.

You've learned the GLOW Method. You've done the work. You've seen what's possible. Now it's time to live it.

Your transformation doesn't end when you close this book. It begins when you decide to apply everything you've learned. It begins when you choose to trust yourself. It begins when you decide to glow anyway.

The woman you're becoming is ready. She's been ready. She's just been waiting for you to believe in her.

So believe in her. Trust her. Let her lead.

And when life gets hard—and it will—remember this moment. Remember that you have everything you need inside you. Remember that you've already survived 100% of your worst days. Remember that your glow is not conditional on your circumstances.

Now go show the world what it looks like when a woman refuses to dim her light.

Go glow anyway.

The stage is yours.

Conclusion

Remember how this book started? With me on my kitchen floor—the empty Jack Daniel's bottle still warm in my hand, my ex's gun on the counter.

That woman thought her story was ending. She believed the darkness had won. She couldn't see past the pain to imagine a different life was possible.

But that night wasn't my ending. It was my invitation.

An invitation to stop running from the truth about who I was and who I could become. An invitation to stop numbing the pain and start healing it. An invitation to stop abandoning myself and start fighting for the woman I knew was buried under all that shame.

If someone had handed me this book that night, if someone had looked me in the eyes and said, "Your glow is not lost, it's just covered," I might have put the gun down sooner. I might have believed that change was possible before I nearly destroyed myself trying to escape the pain.

But maybe I needed to walk through that fire to become the woman who could write these words for you.

Maybe every broken moment, every backslide, every time I thought I'd never figure it out, was preparing me to hand you something I wish I'd had: proof that you can rise from rock bottom and glow anyway.

To the Woman Who Doesn't Think She Has What It Takes

I know you don't feel like you have what it takes. I remember that place. I remember waking up already defeated. Wondering if I'd ever feel different. Wondering if I'd always be stuck doing the same thing, feeling the same pain, living the same loops.

I didn't see strength in myself, either. But here's what I need you to understand:

You don't have to be the strongest woman in the room right now. You don't need to know the whole plan. You don't even need to have it all figured out. You just need one small thing—the tiniest next step.

Drink the water. Take a shower. Step outside and let the sun hit your face. That's it. That's how it starts. Move.

The version of you who feels weak right now? She's carrying more strength than she realizes. She's carrying survival. She's carrying grit. She's carrying the quiet kind of power that's forged in the fire.

Every time you got back up when life knocked you down, that was strength. Every time you kept going when you wanted to quit, that was strength. Every time you chose love over fear, even in small ways, that was strength. Every time you survived a day that felt impossible, that was strength.

You've been building strength your whole life. You just haven't been calling it that.

So don't quit on yourself. You don't have to do it all at once. Just don't stop. Keep moving. Keep breathing. Keep showing up.

Because if I can climb out of that pit—drunk, broken, holding a gun in my hands—so can you. If I can rebuild from nothing, so can you. If I can learn to glow in the middle of the mess, so can you.

This isn't the end of my story. It's the opening of yours. Every page you've read was written to hand you the pen.

What's ahead for you is different than what was ahead for me when I began. I spent years stuck in loops, repeating lies, piecing things together the hard way. You don't have to.

You have the words I didn't. You have proof that healing can be messy and still count. You have permission to shine in the middle of the storm, not just after the skies clear.

Where I fought to survive, you can choose to expand. Where I scraped my way back, you can step forward softer, sooner, freer. You're not starting from scratch. You're starting from here—with tools, with vision, with light already breaking through.

What I Guarantee You

Here's what I can promise you with complete confidence, because I've lived it:

Your glow isn't gone. Not when you're starting over with nothing. Not when you're sleeping on a cot and piecing life together paycheck by paycheck. Not when you're fighting through exhaustion and wondering if you'll ever recognize yourself again. The glow is still there. I know, because I once believed mine was lost for good.

For years, I was convinced the light inside me had been smothered—that the divorce, the setbacks, the long shifts, the choices I regretted had buried it too deep. I thought I was too far behind, too worn down, too unworthy to rise.

But here's the truth: you can't kill what's rooted in your soul. You can bury it under burnout, silence it with self-doubt, numb it with distractions, but you cannot destroy it. That spark is indestructible. And the moment you stop doubting it and start nurturing it, it grows.

You will not stay stuck. Where you are right now is not permanent. I've been the woman convinced she had ruined everything. What felt like rock bottom was actually the ground I needed to push off from.

Pain taught me that growth isn't about staying polished—it's about practicing recovery. Every relapse, every setback, every detour isn't the end of the story—it's feedback. It shows you where to adjust, where to strengthen, where to love yourself harder.

That's where the glow breaks through. Not when life is flawless, but when you stop waiting for perfect conditions and start moving forward with what you have.

Your story is not over. You are allowed to want more. You are allowed to change direction. You are allowed to rise again, and again, and again. You can build a life that feels like home. You can create peace without having to earn it first.

Because the glow doesn't show up after everything is "fixed." It shows up the moment you remember you're worthy of light—even while it's still dark.

If This Book Is the Light Breaking Through

If this book is the light breaking through after the longest night, here's the dawn I'm promising you:

A life that feels different because you feel different.

On the other side, the old lies don't get to run the show. The shame doesn't get the last word. The survival mode that once kept you trapped doesn't get to set the pace anymore.

What becomes possible is trust in yourself. Trusting your voice, your choices, your ability to keep showing up even when it's hard. Trusting that you know what's best for you better than anyone else does.

What becomes possible is peace. The kind that steadies you even when life isn't perfect. The kind that comes from knowing you're living aligned with your values. The kind that doesn't depend on external circumstances.

What becomes possible is joy. Not the kind you have to chase, but the genuine kind you create on ordinary days. The kind that bubbles up from a life that feels authentic and meaningful.

What becomes possible is self-worth. Carrying yourself with respect like you belong because you do. Knowing your value isn't up for negotiation. Setting standards that honor who you're becoming.

You no longer have to run from your life. You get to live in it—fully. The night shaped you, but it doesn't own you. The dawn belongs to you.

What You Don't Have to Do Anymore

Here's what you're officially released from:

You don't have to earn rest. You don't have to prove you deserve a break. You don't have to exhaust yourself to justify taking care of your needs. Rest is not a luxury you earn. It's a necessity you honor.

You don't have to earn joy. You don't have to wait until everything is perfect to be happy. You don't have to fix yourself before you're allowed to enjoy your life. Joy is your birthright, not your reward for good behavior.

You don't have to earn love. You don't have to be perfect to be worthy of affection. You don't have to transform yourself to deserve kindness. You don't have to perform to be valued. You are lovable exactly as you are.

You don't have to earn belonging. You don't have to change yourself to fit in. You don't have to shrink to make others comfortable. You belong in spaces that celebrate who you are, not spaces that require you to be someone else.

You don't have to carry what isn't yours. Other people's emotions, expectations, and limitations are not your responsibility. You can love people without fixing them. You can support people without saving them.

You don't have to explain your choices. Your decisions are yours to make. Your boundaries are yours to set. Your life is yours to live. You don't owe anyone a justification for choosing yourself.

You don't have to stay small to make others comfortable. Your growth might threaten people who benefit from your limitations. That's their issue to work through, not yours to manage.

You don't have to wait for permission to change. You don't need approval to evolve. You don't need consensus to grow. You don't need anyone's blessing to become who you're meant to be.

Nobody told me I could just stop playing by rules that were killing me. Nobody said, "Hey, you can quit that game anytime you want."

I'm telling you now: You can stop anytime you want. The game only has power over you as long as you keep playing.

Your First Assignment

Here's your first assignment as the author of your own story: Write yourself a letter.

Write to the woman you're becoming. Tell her what you're proud of her for. Tell her what you hope she remembers. Tell her what you want her to know about this moment. Tell her how you see her living, loving, and glowing.

Then read it to yourself every morning for the next week. Let those words sink into your bones. Let yourself believe them. Because they're not hopes or wishes or fantasies.

They're truths about who you already are, waiting for you to claim them.

Everything you need is already inside you.

The courage you've been waiting for? It's there. The love you've been seeking? It's there. The wisdom you've been praying for? It's there. The strength you've been questioning? It's there. The glow you've been chasing? It's there.

You don't have to chase it in someone else. You don't have to prove it through perfection. You don't have to beg the world to hand it to you.

It has always been yours. Waiting quietly, patiently, for you to stop doubting and trust yourself enough to claim it.

What I need you to never forget is this: The life you long for doesn't begin "someday." It begins the moment you choose to believe in what's already inside you.

Trust yourself, and the glow becomes unshakable—untouchable by anyone but you.

What Showing Up Raw Looks Like

You asked what showing up raw looks like in a world that rewards perfection. Let me tell you.

Showing up raw means telling the truth about where you are, even when it's uncomfortable. It means saying "I'm struggling" instead of "I'm fine" when someone asks how you're doing. It means admitting when you don't have all the answers.

Showing up raw means feeling your feelings without apology. It means crying when you need to cry, raging when you need to rage, and not rushing to pretty it up for other people's comfort.

Showing up raw means asking for help when you need it. It means admitting you can't do everything alone. It means letting people see you vulnerable and imperfect and human.

Showing up raw means making mistakes and owning them. It means saying "I messed up" instead of making excuses. It means learning from your failures instead of hiding them.

Showing up raw means setting boundaries without over-explaining them. It means saying no when you need to say no and not launching into a dissertation about why.

Showing up raw means pursuing your dreams even when you're scared. It means taking imperfect action instead of waiting until you feel ready. It means trying things you might fail at.

Showing up raw means loving yourself out loud. It means treating yourself with kindness where others can see it. It means modeling self-respect and self-care as revolutionary acts.

In a world that rewards perfection, showing up raw is rebellion. It's refusing to participate in the lie that you have to have it all together to be worthy of love, respect, and belonging.

Raw is real. Raw is honest. Raw is brave.

And raw is exactly how the world needs you to show up.

The Ripple Effect of Your Courage

When you stop hiding, when you decide to live as the woman you've been becoming all along, when you choose truth over expectation—something bigger than you begins to unfold:

You give other people permission to do the same.

Your courage becomes contagious. Your authenticity becomes an invitation. Your glow becomes a lighthouse for someone still lost in the storm.

Every time you choose growth over comfort, you plant the seed of possibility in someone else. You show them that it's okay to outgrow old rooms, old relationships, and old versions of themselves. You give them a living example that change doesn't have to be loud to be powerful—it can start with one quiet decision.

Every time you hold a boundary without apology, you model self-respect for someone who's never seen it done. You demonstrate that saying "no" doesn't make you difficult—it makes you clear. You show that protecting your peace isn't selfish—it's essential. And in doing so, you give others permission to value themselves enough to draw their own lines.

Every time you get back up after a fall, you rewrite the story of what resilience looks like. You prove that setbacks aren't the end—they're the training ground. You remind others that stumbling doesn't cancel the progress they've made—it strengthens it. By rising, you show them that resilience isn't about never falling; it's about refusing to stay down.

This is how cycles break. This is how families heal. This is how communities transform. This is how the world changes.

One woman at a time. One choice at a time. One glow at a time.

Not through perfection. Through practice. Through persistence. Through ordinary women choosing extraordinary honesty, one decision at a time.

And your healing? It matters. Not just for you—but for every woman who comes after you. For your daughters and their daughters. For the women in your family line who never had the chance to choose differently. For the ones watching you now, wondering if they're allowed to want more.

You are the proof. You are the evidence. You are the ripple.

Your story doesn't end here. It begins here.

Because when one woman steps into her power, she opens the door for all of us.

The Invitation

So here's my invitation to you:

Come raw. Show up exactly as you are, messy and imperfect and still figuring it out. Don't wait until you have it all together. Don't wait until you feel ready. Don't wait until you feel worthy. Come now, as you are.

Come willing. Willing to do the hard work of growth. Willing to feel uncomfortable emotions. Willing to face truths you've been avoiding. Willing to try things that might not work. Willing to become someone new.

Glow anyway. Glow in the middle of your chaos. Glow while you're still healing. Glow while you're still learning. Glow while you're still becoming. Don't wait for perfect conditions to let yourself shine.

How I Can Walk With You

If you're ready to go deeper, if you want support as you write this new chapter, if you want a guide who's walked this path and can help you navigate yours, I'm here.

My coaching program is designed for women who are done living small and ready to step into their power. Women who want to break patterns, heal trauma, and design lives they don't want to escape from. Women who are ready to glow anyway.

In my program, you'll get:

- The complete GLOW Method with step-by-step implementation
- Group coaching calls where you can ask questions and get support
- A community of women who are on the same journey
- Resources and tools to help you maintain your momentum
- My personal guidance as you navigate your transformation

You don't have to do this alone. You don't have to figure it out by yourself. You can have support, community, and guidance as you become the woman you're meant to be.

If you're interested in learning more, scan the QR code below or visit my website. Your transformation is waiting.

As you close this book and step into your new story, I want to leave you with this promise:

I believe in you. I believe in your strength, your resilience, your capacity for growth. I believe you have everything inside you that you need to create a life you love.

I believe your best days are ahead of you, not behind you. I believe your story is just getting started. I believe your glow is going to light up the world.

And when you doubt yourself—and you will—come back to these pages. Read them again. Remember who you are. Remember what you're capable of. Remember that you are worthy of every good thing you desire.

Now go show the world what it looks like when a woman refuses to dim her light.

Go write the story only you can write.

Go live the life only you can live.

Come raw. Come willing. Glow anyway.

Your story starts now.

The End... and The Beginning

www.ingramcontent.com/pod-product-compliance
Lightning Source LLC
LaVergne TN
LVHW050617100826
845148LV00011B/1623

* 9 7 9 8 2 1 8 8 2 4 8 9 1 *